The Impact of the

HOLY SPIRIT

on Mortal Man

Dr. Joe R. Williams, Sr.

TATE PUBLISHING, LLC

ABSTRACT

This book is a biblical and theological study of the human response that occurs in connection with manifestations of God's presence. By investigating the human response, we are ultimately interested in how God's spirit, or presence, affects mankind, and how this understanding can better inform our theological understanding of the character and nature of God and man.

The study consists of six chapters, organized in salvation-historical sequence from Genesis to Revelation. With the exception of the introductory and concluding chapters, each chapter treats a specific biblical time period and offers significant theological observations.

The first period of interest centers on Eden, which includes the creation of man in the image of God, life in the garden of God's presence, and the fall and its subsequent effects on the first couple. Post-fall divine encounters with God are then examined at Sinai and in other contexts of the Pentateuch. This will lead one to understand the significance of the human response and development within the context of redemptive history. The focus then turns to God's divine presence with Israel's Tabernacle and Temple in the periods

of conquest and kingdom. A consideration of the major em-
phases and theological significance of the human response to
God's presence in the Old Testament is set forth before consideration of the responses to God's presence in the person
of Christ, followed by the advent of God's divine presence
at Pentecost, and the subsequent growth of the New Testament church.

The next section treats culmination and renewal
in the eschaton, toward which all previous redemptive-
historical events were but a foreshadowing and foretaste.
In the final section I will attempt to synthesize the various
chapters in the form of some helpful concluding points.

ACKNOWLEDGMENTS

It is my pleasant duty to express gratitude to those who prayed and supported me in writing this book. Special thanks are in order to the Lord for His goodness and mercy. Thanks to my children and their spouses, Angie Hankins, Pamela Richard (Michael), Lakesha Williams, Joe R. Williams Jr (Carisma), Ronald Williams (Charity), and Joshua Williams (Ke'Ell) for their encouragement and love. Thank you, Andrew and Doris Williams, my parents who taught me about life. Thanks to my Father in the Gospel, Suffragan Bishop Charles W. Meadows, who taught and inspired me down through the years. Thank you, American Bible College and Seminary for treating my work and me with great dignity. Thank you, True Love Apostolic Faith Church Family, for your compassion and encouragement. Above all, I am deeply grateful to my wife, Treddie Jean Williams, for her constant prayers, patience, and loving support throughout this whole endeavor. Treddie, who I call my chocolate cake, is a gift from God.

TABLE OF CONTENTS

Foreword

This writer has known Dr. Williams for close to four years and has had the pleasure of preaching from the pulpit of the church he serves in Lawton. From this association came the knowledge of Dr. Williams' concern for the impact that the Holy Spirit has upon Christian character development. Williams, therefore, offers a look at the person and work of the Holy Spirit from an angle other than the strictly theological, doctrinal, or psychological without ignoring any of the aforementioned. The power of the Holy Spirit upon personality and character development is of critical importance, affecting both personal holiness and community outreach. Personal holiness does not consist in what a person does or does not do or in simply being a good person. Holiness has to do with character and personality development and the making of a person whose life radiates the love and grace of God toward those around him or her.

From this point the Holy Spirit works outward from the person to have impact upon integrity of person, ethical decision-making in both the private and public squares, and in community outreach. The Christian whose life has been affected by the Holy Spirit becomes automatically a public person so affected knowing it. That life is on display.

Williams' work is to be highly commended as it seeks to reach beyond the theological and the doctrinal to the practical outworking of the Holy Spirit within the life of individual Christians as they live out their lives and in the life, work, and missionary outreach of the church.

Woodrow E. Walton, D. Min.
Norman, Oklahoma
December 2005

Chapter One

INTRODUCTION

The subject of God drawing near to humans is a central theme within the Bible's storyline. Whether the picture is one portraying the free and open fellowship the first couple shared with Yahweh in the Garden of Eden, or of the throne of God and of the Lamb dwelling in the midst of the inhabitants of the New Jerusalem, instances of God's manifest presence permeate every stratum of the biblical record.

The Purposes of this Study

The purpose of this book is to examine the biblical data regarding human response in connection with God's manifest presence. By investigating human response phenomena, the interest is in how God's presence affects the subjects of his self-disclosure. And as will be observed in the concluding chapter, such a study has value for the life of the church and contributes to theological discourse.

The subject entails several considerations. First, even a cursory glance at the biblical data suggests that a manifestation of God's presence to man is no small or subsidiary topic within Scripture. In fact, every divine self-disclosure in Scripture appears to affect human response. Thus, observing the various human responses involved with manifestations of God's presence can often aid understanding of the purposes for God's self-disclosures in Scripture.

A second but related consideration is that the various human responses recorded in Scripture communicated important theological implications about God and man. For example, at times God's presence may result in humans trembling. Theologically, we face the challenge of determining why the biblical texts record such response, where they fit within the flow of redemptive history, and how they are viewed within that history.[1] Such an inquiry will not only better our understanding of the relevant texts on the exegetical level, but will also build a basis for a theological judgment on what actually happened; and, in short, suggest how these responses are to be evaluated.

A third consideration has to do with occasional claims to a heightened activity of God's manifest presence throughout church history, and particularly during the 21st century. Participants maintain that this activity is frequently attended by strong human responses in both Christians and non-Christians. Understandably, such claims have attracted critics, defenders, and no small amount of questions. A careful theological examination of this subject can help to establish a biblical starting point for discussion of the topic, which may in turn help moderate excessive views. However, my goal is to offer helpful, descriptive observations that shed light on this biblical subject, rather than to arrive at normative prescription for the life and worship of the church.[2]

Fourth, and finally, no significant biblical research exists on this particular subject. Although scant research in itself does not warrant the study, it does help establish the need to investigate this area of biblical revelation particularly if the project could prove helpful to the theological community and benefit the church of Jesus Christ at large.

Structure and Limitations

The study consists of six chapters, organized in salvation-historical sequence from Genesis to Revelation. Each chapter treats a specific biblical time period and offers significant theological observations. In the final chapter, a synthesis is attempted with some helpful conclusions.

The limitations for this study are several. First, the data under consideration are those biblical instances where a manifestation of God's presence resulted in human response. Emotional responses will be an object of consideration only when they closely correspond to human responses.

Second, although physical healings may be viewed as legitimate human responses to God's manifest presence (and indeed as precursors to full eschatological restoration), they are excluded from this present study since the subject is so encompassing and, thus, ought to be examined separately. The same limitation is true for spiritual gifts and manifestations. Focus is on spontaneous human response as they occur within the contexts of Scriptural account.

Third, we have also excluded any human response resulting from angelic and demonic manifestations. Although these data are of interest for comparative purposes, in this study they are peripheral and unessential.

Chapter Two

CONSIDERATIONS
FROM EDEN

Introduction

The book of Genesis is an appropriate starting point for a serious study of nearly any major biblical doctrine. Genesis is a word derived from the Septuagint (the Greek version of the Old Testament) and means "origin" or "beginning." As the "book of beginnings," Genesis constitutes an indispensable introduction to the entire Bible. It forms the foundation of all revealed truth. The key word of Genesis is election. Divine electing grace pervades the book. Important beginnings described are 1) *the beginning of the earth as man's habitation (Genesis 1:1–2:3)*; 2) *the beginning of the human race (Genesis 2:7–25)*; 3) *the beginning of human sin (Genesis 3:1–8)*; 4) *the beginning of redemptive revelation (Gen. 3:9–24); 5) the beginning of the human family (Genesis 4:1–15); 6) the beginning of civilization (Genesis 4:16–9:29)*; 7) *the beginning of nations (Genesis 10:1–32)*; 8) *the beginning of human languages (Genesis 11:1–9)*; 9) *the beginning of the Hebrew race (Genesis 11:10–50:26)*.

Several key salvation-historical events within the early stages of redemptive history occur in the early chapters of Genesis. Without question, these events are a backdrop for significant themes that pervade the rest of the Old Testament (OT) and the New Testament (NT). Prominent among such themes are creation, covenantal relationship, sin, and the fall. Each theme is theologically interrelated with the others, and is rooted in the early chapters of Genesis. These issues and many others are chronicled in this book in order to provide answers to life's most basic questions.

The aim of this chapter is, first, to focus attention on two important events in the history of salvation—the creation of man as image of God, and the fall of man into sin. Toward that end, considerable attention will be given to *Genesis 1:26–27,* as well as the fall of man in *Genesis 3:1–24.* These two events are crucial components of the Bible's own unfolding storyline. Thus, present concerns are both biblical and theological.

As a second aim, the theological significance of human responses to God's manifest presence in the pre- and post- fall biblical contexts will be respectively discussed. Theological implications arising from these points will be of particular interest.

Genesis 1:26—Man as the "Image and Likeness of God"

The importance of the creation of man in the early portions of *Genesis 1:26* is seen both in the larger literary structure of Genesis, as well as by the narrower literary context surrounding these verses.

Genesis 1:26–27 marks the first biblical reference to man—particularly within the context of the created order. Recognition of the larger parallel structure and progression in Genesis chapter one, as well as the internal structure represented by the various formulas, is indispensable to a proper understanding of the material in *Genesis 1:26.* For example, on the larger structural level, it clearly stands as the culminating expression of God's creative work. In short, man is the final and crowning work of God's creative activity. Furthermore, considering the pronouncement formula at man's creation in *Genesis 1:28–29,* one might even conclude that the previous acts of creation had been in anticipation, and on behalf, of the creation of man. Man was made last of all the creatures. It was both an honor and favor to him. Man, as soon as he was made, had the whole visible creation before him, both to contemplate and in which to take comfort. Man's creation was a more signal and immediate act of divine wisdom and power than that of the other creatures. It has been said, "Let there be light," "Let there be a firmament," and "Let the earth, or waters, bring forth"; but now the word of command is turned into a word of consultation, "Let us make man." Man was so important that God said, "This is a work we must take into our own hands." He speaks as one having authority and affection. Man was to be a creature different from all that had been made. Flesh and spirit, heaven and earth, must be put together in him, and he must be allied to both worlds. It pleased God to make man in his own image.

Man was made in God's image. Christ only is the express image of God's person, as the Son of his Father, having the same nature. It is only some of God's honor that is put upon man, who is God's image only as the shadow in the glass, or the King's impress upon the coin.

God's image upon man consists of three things: 1) in his nature and constitution, not those of his body (for God has not a body), but those of his soul. God has indeed put this honor upon the body of man, that the Word was made flesh, the Son of God was clothed with a body like ours and will shortly clothe ours with glory like that of his. The soul of man is considered in three noble faculties: understanding, will and active power, which is perhaps the brightest, clearest looking glass in nature wherein to see God.

2) Man was God's representative upon earth. His government of himself by the freedom of his will has in it

more of God's image than his government of the creatures. God's image upon man consists in knowledge, righteousness, and true holiness, *Ephesians 4:24*.

Among the creation to which God gave the "breath of life," man is clearly distinct in many ways. Furthermore, the creation of man brings new and informative changes to the wording of the creation narrative.

God created man in his image, only to have this godly image deteriorate to an idol of self indulgence (*Genesis 1:27; 9:6*). Scriptures are very clear regarding the creation of man. The Lord God formed man out of the dust of the ground and breathed into his nostrils the breath of life. Man was God's highest act of creation and was in God's own likeness. The image of God refers to the moral and intellectual nature of man. Man was created sinless with an absolute purity and holiness. He was clothed with the righteousness of God until he disobeyed. This disobedience caused man to realize that he was naked. The intellectual nature of man proves that he is not evolved from a lower order but was created in the image of his Creator.

3) Man was given the intelligence necessary to name all living creatures and have dominion over this earth (*Genesis 2:19–20*). He was given the power to reason and to make decisions, and was given a free will as a moral agent. God granted man the option to make the wrong decision and sin in the original transgression. Man is important in God's eyesight. This receives scriptural support in *Hebrews 2:6–8,* which says, *"What is man that thou are mindful of him? Or the son of man, that thou visit him?"*

An Interrelationship of the Aspects of the Image of God

Each of the constituent aspects that make up man's being is interconnected with the others at a fundamental level. Consequently, man's interaction with the spiritual world can affect him physically, just as his interaction with the physical world can affect him spiritually. The point is that man, originally created in God's image and likeness, was simply a representation of God on Earth. The process of salvation is the restoration of that image, bringing man back to the place where he harmonizes with God's presence in every aspect of his being. *St. John 2:19 and I Corinthians 6:19* inform that our body is the temple of God, where God's presence dwells. We are not our own, but bought with a price–the precious blood of Jesus. God is to be glorified in our bodies and our spirit, which both belong to God.

Man, as the image of God, has the capacity to respond to God's presence with every aspect of his being. Consequently, the greatest command in Scripture reads: *"Love the Lord your God with all your heart and with all your soul and with all your mind and with all your strength"* (*St. Mark 12:30; cf Deuteronomy 6:5; St. Matthew 22:37; St. Luke 10:27*). In practical terms, this means that man has the capacity to love and respond to God not only in the context of prayer and worship, but in his work, leisure, and family relationships, and can do so with his whole being.

Conversely, it is also possible for God's communication to affect every part of man's being, be it spiritually (granting spiritual peace with God), emotionally (prompting joy, sorrow, anger, or fear in God-ordained times and ways), mentally (prompting thoughts that establish loving attitudes toward God, neighbor, and the world), or physically (prompting physical acts of worship and service according to His will).[3] Each of these examples illustrates positive effects involving human cooperation. The impact of God's presence can also result in effects both unexpected and independent of human volition or desire.

Manifestation of God's presence in the Garden

The remainder of the second chapter of Genesis contains further descriptions of this "garden of delight." Essential to Eden as a garden of blessings was the manifestation of God's presence, which proved to be the true source of all blessing and provision. After God created the man, He placed him in the midst of the garden with the declared purpose, "to work it and take care of it" (*Genesis. 2:15*).

The theological difficulties with the traditional rendering "to work it and take care of it" are not very substantial. Although it is acknowledged that toilsome labor is a consequence of the fall. The context of God's blessing on the man's work in the garden makes such activity qualitatively different. This "work" prior to the fall involved no curse on the ground. Consequently, there would be no "painful toil," "thorns and thistles," or "sweat of your face" to make this work a drudgery (*Genesis 3:17–19*). Instead, man was free to exercise his faculties and creative energies in the presence of his Creator.

Furthermore, through the activity of work we see one more example of the man reflecting the image of his Creator. For just as God had engaged in the work of creation (*Genesis 2:2*), and indeed, still works to this day, so also man was called to reflect God's creative activity in work, employing and developing his faculties to the glory of God. An example of such work is seen even in the post-fall context of *Exodus 35:30–33*.

The Tree of Life and the Tree of the Knowledge of Good and Evil

After creating the man "from the dust of the ground" (*Genesis 2:7*), and placing him in a garden that the Lord planted, there is a clear reference to God's life-sustaining provision and care for the man in the form of the diverse types of trees that were "pleasing to the eye and good for food" (2:9). Among these trees were the tree of life and the tree of the knowledge of good and evil, each planted in the middle of the garden.

The text records that the Lord God came to the man and extended a free invitation to partake of all the trees in the garden, except for the tree of the knowledge of good and evil (2:16–17). Although the man had open access to this tree, its fruit was forbidden on the threat of capital sanctions. The tree of life, in contrast, was God's designated means whereby the man's life would be sustained forever.

The Naming of the Animals

According to the text, God also manifested his presence to bring the various beasts of the ground and birds of the air that he had formed before Adam. Man responded to God's action by speaking a name for the animal in God's presence, and "whatever the man called a living creature, that was its name" (*Genesis 2:19*). Adam's response to God's action was an example of his bearing the image and likeness of God.

Without Shame in God's Presence

As if to capture a picture of the blessed harmony that existed in the garden prior to the Fall, the final verse in Genesis chapter two states: *"The man and his wife were both naked, and they felt no shame"* (*Genesis 2:25*). Consequently, this phrase sums up the first man and woman's life in the garden of God's presence. There was perfect harmony and blissful innocence. As we shall observe later in the context of the fall, this final statement in chapter two not only indicates that the first couple was unaware of their nakedness, but is also descriptive of how they were without shame and guilt in the manifest presence of God.

Theological Significance of Man's Life in the Garden for Human Responses to God's Manifest Presence

In the absence of sin, God's presence was man's natural abode, his true place of "rest" [4] among the many blessings of the garden. Furthermore, God's presence was the catalyst and context whereby man reflected God's glory as the image of God. This reflection is evident in the garden, where he responded to God's presence by employing his faculties in creative work. Work, as originally intended, was a reflex-response of God's image in man.

Moreover, God's invitation for the man to eat the various fruit of the trees, and from the tree of life in particular, served as an external sign of man's free and unrestricted access into God's presence, the source of all life. When the man partook of the tree on the physical level, he was, in fact, partaking of God's presence. The trees were at some level sacramental. As we shall see in the context of the fall, when the woman and the man ate the forbidden fruit, they had, in fact, chosen another life-source in the place of God. They fell out of God's Divine Will into his Permissive Will.

Still another example where God's presence served as a catalyst to illuminate the image of God in man is seen when the Lord brings first the animals, and later the woman before the man. As already noted, the man's response to God with speech uniquely demonstrates his similitude to God. Man was actually speaking and not just uttering meaningless sounds as "names." This is evident in the full narrative of why he chose the name "Woman," when God brought the female before him: *"This is now bone of my bones, and flesh of my flesh; She shall be called Woman, because she was taken out of man"* (*Genesis 2:23 KJV*). This explanation includes grammar, syntax and vocabulary—necessary components in speech.

Consequently, these responses to God's presence in the garden reveal a harmony of free and open fellowship with their Creator that is unobstructed and pure. For this reason, therefore, the Scripture declares, *"And God saw all that he had made, and behold, it was very good"* (*Genesis 1:31 KJV*).

Genesis 3 The Interruption of God's Blessing by Sin

Attempts in the history of interpretation to find textual evidence for the effects of the fall on the image of God were not entirely misguided. Clearly, something happened to the human race after the first man and woman chose to disobey God.

Satan, at length, gains his point, and the stronghold is taken by his wiles. In *Genesis 3:1–3*, the serpent's deceit leads to the fall of Adam and Eve. The presence of God did not leave man until he ate the fruit, *"then both of their eyes were opened, and they realized they were naked; so they sewed fig leaves together and made covering for themselves." (Genesis 3:6–7).* Their hearts smote them for what they had done. They lost their joy and happiness and became miserable because of sin. They were stripped, deprived of all the honors and joys of their paradise. They hid themselves from the presence of God. Their behavior changed from enjoying the presence of God to not caring any more, and from good to evil. Adam and Eve's new perception of their relationship with God caused them to become terror to themselves. Their own consciences accused them and set their sin before them in its proper colors. Their figs leaves failed them and would do them no service.

The serpent promised them that they will be safe, but now they cannot so much as think themselves so; he promised them they should be knowing, but they see themselves at a loss and know not so much as where to hide themselves; he promised them they should be as gods, great, bold and daring, but they are criminals discovered. Sin can't hide from God, and it must be punished. Man lost fellowship with God and contaminated the whole earth.

The serpent thought he was interrupting God's plan for good, but it was just for a season. Even though man stepped out of the presence of God, the Creator still had mercy on mankind. He gave mankind a promise of a Redeemer before he mentioned to them the consequences they would have to pay for their sins. In *Genesis 3:15,* we have the first promise of the Messiah, *"I will put enmity between thee and the woman, and between thy seed and her seed; it shall bruise thy head, and thy shall bruise his heel."* The Seed of the woman is Jesus, for he was born of a virgin. Satan "bruised his heel" or stopped his walking for three days while in the tomb. When he arose triumphant over death, Christ bruised the serpent head and he bought man back from the bondage of Satan. God loved man so much that he made a way for Jesus to die. Jesus shed his blood so man could come back into the presence of God.

The whole story of the first sin in *Genesis 3* is rooted in the shaking of faith in God and His word. It is apparent from the narrative that the root of mankind's sin and ensuing fall is unbelief. Rather than standing upon God's word in faith, the man and the woman departed from it. Sin thus entered upon the world when mankind turned from God and His word. Man was drawn away by Satan, who long before attempted to exalt himself from the position that God had given him. Pride always tries to exalt itself above its created position. *"Pride goes before destruction, and a haughty spirit before a fall"* (*Proverbs 16:18 KJV*). The temptation to Eve was to become "like God." Man was not made to play God; he was made to worship Him.

Disobedience is not the beginning of the fall, but its fruition is in the will. The progression as observed in the scriptural account of the fall is from unbelief to pride to disobedience. Sin in its true essence, therefore, is the deliberate act of disobedience.

Theological Significance of the Fall for Human Responses to God's Manifest Presence

We may conclude with good evidence, therefore, that *Genesis 3:8* is a salvation-historical God who is seen in various future manifestations of God's glory. Noteworthy in this Genesis narrative, however, are the attending effects that both the fall and God's manifestation had upon the man and the woman.

Fear and Shame:

Most immediate and direct is a response of fear and shame. Adam and Eve hid from the Lord God among the trees of the garden, as well as in the man's response to the Lord God, "I heard you in the garden, and I was afraid because I was naked; so I hid" (3:10).

The connection between the couple's participation in the tree of the knowledge of good and evil, and a definitive shift in ethical perception or moral experience is explicit at this point. The key in this term is the recognition that they were "naked." This is a condition, which, prior to the fall, the text explicitly states engendered no sense of shame in either person (2:25). In fact, the man and the woman were created in the image and likeness of God; a condition, as we have seen, that is quite the opposite of fear and shame. Undoubtedly, the recurrence of nakedness in both pre- and post-fall contexts serves to highlight its use as a descriptive gauge for the condition of their relationship with God and with one another. Note the way nakedness appears in these contexts:

Pre-Fall State:
    "The man and his wife were both naked, and they felt no shame." Genesis 2:25

Post-Fall State:
    Then the eyes of both of them were opened, and they realized they were naked: so they sewed fig leaves together and made coverings for themselves." Genesis 3:7

    "I heard you in the garden, and I was afraid because I was naked; so I hid." Genesis 3:10

"Who told you that you were naked? Have you eaten from the tree that I commanded you not to eat from?" Genesis 3:11

The fact that the Lord God takes the initiative to replace the man and woman's leaf covering with skin garments through the death of some type of animal may prefigure the future removal of mankind's nakedness before God through Christ, God's own sacrificial lamb (3:21). The author of the New Testament letter to the Hebrews certainly saw strong type/antitype connections when comparing the Levitical sacrificial system and the ultimate sacrifice of Christ on the cross, and writes, *"Without the shedding of blood there is no remission of sins" (Hebrews 9:22 KJV).*

In the context of Genesis, therefore, it is fair to conclude that the knowledge of good and evil is nothing less than an awareness ("the eyes of both of them were opened,") [*Genesis 3:7*]. They were exposed of guilt and shame before the Lord. There are other Scripture passages which communicate this concept of exposure before God with the following metaphors:

"Death is naked before God; Destruction lies uncovered" Job 26:6.

"Meanwhile we groan, long to be clothed with our heavenly dwelling, because when we are clothed, we will not be found naked" II Corinthians 5:2–3.

"Behold, I am coming like a thief. Blessed is the one who stays awake and keeps his garments, lest he walk about naked and men see his shame" Revelation 16:15.

Physical and Spiritual Death

Such exposure also points to another distinct effect of the fall–a relational shift, both on the horizontal level between the man and the woman (*Genesis 3:16*), as well as on the vertical level between man and God. Here we see that Adam and Eve are not only fearfully hiding due to the Lord God's advancing presence in the context of their nakedness, but also because of the knowledge of the very sanction denied by the serpent—death (3:4).

It is hard to reconstruct what this first couple's conception may have been of God's warning of death, but some have questioned whether, in fact, God's warning was fulfilled as he had stated it; namely, "in the day that you eat from the fruit you shall surely die" (2:17). However, a careful reading of the text demonstrates the truthfulness of God's warning, down to the last detail. On the very day that the couple sinned, God pronounced a series of curses, one of which demonstrates that death had already begun to come to them with the words, "By the sweat of your face you will eat your food until you return to the ground, since from it you were taken; for dust you are and to dust you will return" (3:19). Moreover, the banishment of the couple from the tree of life (3:22–24) that same day indicates that a full definition of this term "death" promised earlier by God must also include a major disruption in one's relationship with God's presence. The physical appearance of man states that God is a Spirit and invisible, but it was in the plan and purpose of Deity to manifest himself in the flesh in the incarnation. This incarnation will be manifested through Jesus, the Christ.

It needs to be remembered that as far as time is concerned, the advent of Christ took place at a definite point in history. However, God, who dwells in eternity, saw it from the beginning. There is also a trinity of man. Paul says in *I Thessalonians 5:23, "And the very God of peace sanctify you wholly; and I pray God your whole spirit and soul and body be preserved blameless unto the coming of our Lord*

Jesus Christ" (KJV). Man is body, soul, and spirit. Yet he is one person bearing one name. God has given man unlimited potential. He can rise higher and sink lower than any other of God's creatures.

There seems no bottom to the depths that a man or woman can fall. There also seems to be no limits to the heights that God can lift man. Man has the capacity of yielding to God and becoming a vessel filled with the Spirit of God. *Hebrews 2:6* says, *"Man was crowned with glory and honor and made a little lower than the angels" (KJV).* Man was created neither an ignoramus nor a savage but being of lofty intellectual powers and a high moral nature.

Throughout Genesis chapters 2 and 3, the author has carefully monitored the man's ongoing relationship with his Creator by means of the theme of "eating." At first, God's blessing and provision for man are noted in the words, "you are free to eat from any tree in the garden, but do not eat of the tree of knowledge, which is good and evil: for in the day you eat, you will surely die" (2:16). In chapter 3, it was precisely over the issue of "eating" that the tempter raised doubts about God's ultimate goodness and care for the man and his wife (3:1–3). Finally, the man and the woman's act of disobedience in chapter 3: 6 is simply though thoughtfully described as "she ate it."

In this context, it is not surprising; therefore, that "eating" would also be a part of falling out of God's presence and judgment against the man and woman. In *Genesis. 3:17–19,* God states, *"Cursed is the ground because of you; through painful toil you will eat of it all the days of your life. It will produce thorns and thistles for you, and you will eat the plants of the field. By the sweat of your face, you will eat your food."*

Similarly, in *Genesis 3:22* the Lord God states, *"The man has now become like one of us, knowing good and evil. He must not be allowed to reach out his hand and take also from the tree of life and eat, and live forever."* Later, Levitical food regulations also become a normative means whereby the Israelite community was to walk in covenantal fellowship with God. In this way, eating or partaking in these various instances is an outward symbol (or sacramental means) of the gracious relationship established with their Creator. Scripture abounds with these relational references to eating in various other locations.

Expulsion from God's Manifest Presence

Finally, this introduction of death is complete with an explicit geographical shift–expulsion from the garden or the presence of God. The significance of this change of geography not only centers on God keeping them from the tree of life, but it is much more significant. Scripture suggests of both a geographical location and a description of the manifest blessing of God's presence. Barring the man and the woman from the garden was not only a way of keeping them from the tree of life; the banishment itself barred them from the manifest presence of God and all its attending blessings. As discussed earlier, the results of the Fall had such a cataclysmic impact on the image of God that unreserved freedom in God's manifest presence is not only judicially off limits, but would be extremely unpleasant.[5]

Consequently, with the introduction of sin, the subsequent manifestation of God's presence in the garden resulted in a complete reversal of all of God's previous blessings. Thus the one who was originally placed in the garden "to work and keep it" is now driven away from it (*Genesis 3:24*). The one who was once given free access to all the trees in the garden for food is now barred from the tree of life and must work the cursed ground for his food (3:17–19). The ones who once enjoyed harmony and peace in their relationship of "oneness" must now face discord (3:16). The ones who were exposed to one another and to God in the garden and experienced no shame are now covered with animal skins and filled with guilt and fear before God (3:10). And finally, the ones who were created to live forever are

God's image and likeness must now die and return to the ground from which they were taken (3:19). God's curse upon sin had truly reversed all His previous blessings.

After the fall, man could not approach God, except through a blood covering. The acceptance of Jesus' blood sacrifice is the only thing that brings mankind holiness and righteousness today.

Jesus Christ, who is the express image of God, is a prime example of God's love as reflected through man. Originally, there was nothing that stood in the way of this fellowship, but eventually another freedom that God provided to man caused separation: the freedom of decision.

It is freedom of decision that allows mankind to decide whether or not he or she wants to acknowledge the supreme maker. God would not have it any other way. For if man had no choice or option to make decisions, it would be called something, but not freedom. God wouldn't have it any other way, because who would want something to obey because it has to? The freedom of choice that is granted to mankind is what brings true worship and glory to God. He receives glory out of our choice to obey because of our freedom to make that choice.

The history of salvation is a history of God drawing near to sinful men and women–sometimes in great mercy and grace, sometimes in terrible judgment. The manner in which humans have responded to God's presence can provide us with a great deal of theological insight into the nature of God and the nature of his redemptive activity among fallen men and women. Accordingly, it is apparent why these first three chapters of Genesis were so crucial to setting the stage for an investigation of this nature.

Chapter Three

SINAI AND OTHER
PENTATEUCHAL MANIFESTATIONS

The Ten Commandments lay at the very center of this covenant and on this account became Israel's fundamental law. Here were the basic ethical precepts which, according to Christ's interpretation, resolved man's five manifold duties to two: love to God and love to one's neighbor (*St. Matthew 22:36–40*). With deep understanding, Jesus quoted *Deuteronomy 6:4–5* as defining this love to God. He said, *"You shall love the Lord your God with all your heart, and with all your soul and with all your might."*

The covenant relation of God and Israel naturally led to God's provision for worship. The fleeting vision of God and of the eating of the fellowship meal by the elders of Israel on Sinai pointed the way to similar privileges for all Israel. Accordingly, *God said, "And let them make me a sanctuary, that I may dwell in their midst" (Exodus 25:8 KJV)*. This tabernacle was to be pitched in the midst of the camp of Israel. Its location was a perpetual reminder of Israel's supreme spiritual privilege—God's presence dwelling in their midst. Though He was dwelling among them, Israel's access to His presence was to be severely restricted.

God was teaching the people how they might come into his presence for worship. It was bound up in the word "holy." Five times God said, *"You shall be holy; for I the Lord your God am holy."(Leviticus 11:44, 45; 19:2; 20:7, 26 KJV).* This truth contrasts God's ethical purity with the vileness of man. When Isaiah heard the seraphim calling one to another, "Holy, holy, holy is the Lord of hosts," he saw himself a man of unclean lips and out of the presence of God (*Isaiah 6:3–6*). God's command is, "You shall be holy*" (KJV).* The first context was sins that separated Israel from God. The others are embedded in the so-called "Law of Holiness," within which are specific teachings on the proper conduct of the people of God. God wants us to consecrate ourselves so his presence can remain with us. *God says, "Consecrate yourselves therefore, and be holy" (Leviticus 11:44*). To "consecrate" is to set one's self apart or to someone else. As such, it did not have a moral connotation. We may think of this as its formal sense. But when this separating was unto God, the word took on an ethical meaning and God's presence was very strong.

Exodus 33:5–23 tells how important it is to have the presence of God. In verse 4, the Lord says to Moses, *"Say unto the children of Israel, ye are a stiff-necked people: I will come up into the midst of thee in a moment, and consume thee: therefore now put off thy ornaments from thee, that I may know what to do unto thee."* As Moses entered into the tabernacle, all the people rose up and stood every man at his tent door and looked after Moses until he was gone into the tabernacle. After Moses entered into the tabernacle, the people saw the cloudy pillar (the presence of God) standing at the door. The impact of the presence of God was so powerful that the children of Israel rose up and worshipped, every man at his tent door.

In *Exodus 34:1,* the Lord called Moses to the mountain for forty days and gave him the Ten Commandments.

When Moses came down from the mountain, the presence of the Lord was so strong upon him that he had to put on a veil. The people couldn't stand to look upon him because of the glory of God. God wanted his people to be so caught up in his presence and to love him only. Later in that chapter, the Lord told Moses to get down from the mountain because the people had sinned. Moses went down from the mountain and met Joshua at the bottom. When they arrived, the people were drinking, dancing and worshipping an idol calf. God got so angry with them that he asked the question, "Who's on the Lord side?" The Lord destroyed them because they were disobedient and serving idols.

Numbers 11:25–29 says, "And the Lord came down in a cloud, and spoke unto Moses, and took of the spirit that was upon him, and gave it unto the seventy elders: and it came to pass, that, when the spirit rested upon them, they prophesied, and did not stop. But there remained two of the men in the camp, the name of the one was Eldad, and the other Medad: and the spirit rested upon them, and they stayed in the Tabernacle and prophesied in the camp. And Moses said he wish all God people were prophets and that God would put his spirit upon them" (KJV).

This passage shows us how God's spirit brings about a change in our behavior. The children of Israel were stiff-necked and disobedient. Moses knew the importance of God's spirit moving because it would bring about change in their behavior. [6]

The spirit of the Lord came upon Balaam, Azariah, and Jahaziel (*Numbers 24:2; II Chronicles 15:1; 20:15*). Ezra, reflecting on God's dealing with Israel, said, "Thou gavest thy good Spirit to instruct them" (*Nehemiah 9:20*). David, recognizing the Spirit as an Instructor, prayed, "Teach me to do thy will, for thou art my God! Let thy good Spirit lead me on a level path!" (*Psalm 143:10*). He was aware also of how God searched and knew him. He saw that it was impossible to escape from the presence of the Spirit (*Psalm 139:1–18*). Men refuse to take heed to the

Spirit's warning. Ezra lamented that God had warned Israel during their wanderings by His Spirit through the prophets, yet they would not give ear (*Nehemiah 9:30*). Isaiah also spoke of how Israel *"rebelled and grieved his holy spirit"* (*Isaiah. 63:10*). *"They made their hearts like adamant lest they should hear the law and the words which the Lord of hosts had sent by his Spirit through the former prophets"* (*Zechariah. 7:12 KJV*).

David described his own experience by saying, *"The Spirit of the Lord speaks by me, and his word is upon my tongue"* (*II Samuel 23:2KJV*). Micah exclaimed, *"But as for me, I am filled with power, with the Spirit of the Lord, and with justice and might"* (*Micah 3:8 KJV*). *"This is the word of the Lord to Zerubbabel: Not by might, nor by power, but by my Spirit, says the Lord of hosts"* (*Zechariah 4:6 KJV*). The Spirit of God took possession of Zechariah and said, *"You will not prosper, because ye have forsaken the commandments of the Lord"* (*II Chronicles. 24:20 KJV*). Ezekiel made frequent reference to the activities of the Spirit. The Spirit entered into him and lifted him up, taking him here and there for special work (*Ezekiel 2:2; 3:12, 14; 8:3; 11:1, 24*).

Ezekiel is ordered to prophesy to the wind (Holy Spirit), so he prophesied as he was commanded to the dead bones, which were called Israel. The dead bones lived by a power that went along with the Word of God, which he preached. The dead bones were made to live in answer to prayer, for a spirit of life entered into them. Ezekiel let us know that God's spirit can raise even the driest of bones to life. God's grace can save souls without preaching. The wonderful effects of these means are to obey God. When troubles continue, hopes are often frustrated. Nothing but an active faith in the power, promise, and providence of God will keep them from dying away.

Finally Haggai gave strong encouragement to the leaders of his time by quoting God as saying, *"My Spirit abides among you; fear not"* (*Haggai 2:5 KJV*).

When the spirit of God comes in, it gives direction and guidance. The spirit of God comes to bless you or curse you. The spirit of God will have such an impact on man that when it comes in, he will automatically worship and praise the Lord. The covenant with Israel was a manifestation of God's holiness. God manifested Himself in the majesty of holiness to Israel. He proceeded to require Israel to be holy. Israel's holiness had to do with prohibitions against neglecting the poor, stealing, oppression of neighbors, injustice, hating of neighbors, adultery, etc. God demands and always wills for man to be sanctified, consecrated, cleansed and pure. These covenants show the progression of God's presence—the encounter and impact on man.

The Standard of Holiness in the Psalms

The penitential psalms of David depicted the standard of holiness in the Old Testament. *Psalm 32* is a model for confession. Confession is the only way to gain forgiveness from God. In *Psalm 51,* David acknowledged the depths of the sinfulness of sin in his cry for mercy. Here is seen the nature of the purifying process. It is a washing from iniquity and cleansing from sin. It is a purging with hyssop. It requires the creating of a clean heart and the renewing of a right spirit within. Job had earlier cried, *"If I wash myself with snow, and cleanse my hands with lye, yet thou wilt plunge me into a pit"* (*Job 9:30 KJV*).

The spiritual washing and cleansing had to effect a change in David's inward being. He desired God to teach him wisdom in his secret heart. The cure was recreating and renewing, an act peculiarly God's. The recreating work had to take place in the heart and spirit. We would say that David's "heart" meant the whole inner man. It was used for the mind and understanding, for the will, for the affections, for the conscience, for the motives, for the whole soul. The heart was regarded as the seat of the emotions, passions, and appetites. Thus the radical corruption of human nature was associated with the heart. It was spoken of as uncircumcised, hardened, evil, perverse, godless, deceitful, and desperately corrupt (*Jeremiah 9:26; Ezekiel 4:21; Proverbs 26:23; Job 36:13; Jeremiah 17:9*).

David humbly recognized that sin had worked untold ruin in his heart. His condition required a creative work such as God alone could perform. God would need to give him new, steadfast spirit. David pleaded that God will not cast him away from his presence nor take his Holy Spirit from him. In his prayer, he recognized that God's creative and renewing work was through God's Spirit. Only through such work could the joy of God's salvation be restored to him.

Here, for the first time in Scripture, the God's Spirit was viewed as the agent of spiritual cleansing. The psalmists and the prophets regarded cleansing, purifying, sanctifying, and making holy as distinctively the work of God's Spirit. The manner of the Spirit's encounter with man described earlier confirms this conclusion. This fact furnishes the key to man's achieving holiness—it is not by man's power, but by the Spirit of God.

What a picture of spiritual cleansing! The condition required for it was nothing less than a broken spirit, a broken and contrite heart (*Isaiah 57:15*). What David was willing to do, the nation of Judah refused to do. The divine arraignment found in Isaiah fairly blistered with stern denunciation. The people of Judah were rebellious; they were laden with iniquity; they were the offspring of evildoers; they were sons who dealt corruptly. *Isaiah 1:18* says, *"Come now, let us reason together, says the Lord. Though your sins are like scarlet, they shall be as white as snow; though they are red as crimson, they shall be like wool."*

If we make ourselves clean by repentance and reformation, God will make us white by a full remission. We must be willing and obedient, and we shall eat the good of the land—the land of promise. If sin were pardoned, creature-comforts become comforts indeed. The children of

Israel could not in reason expect any other than that, if they continued obstinate in their disobedience, the sentence of the law should be executed upon them.

Chapter Four

RESPONSES TO THE
MANIFESTATIONS OF THE PRESENCE OF
GOD IN THE PERSON OF CHRIST

Introduction

With the close of the post-exilic prophets, the intervening period to New Testament history is often described as the "four hundred silent years," or intertestamental period, because of the lack of written prophetic revelation. As observed earlier, this period was marked by turmoil and the foreign domination of Palestine by neighboring nations, with repeated destruction of the temple in Jerusalem. Consequently, a second temple was built by the exiles to replace Solomon's, which was destroyed by Nebuchadnezzar (537 B.C.). A third one was built by Herod (19 B.C.) to replace the second destroyed by Pompey (63 B.C.). The Israelites' persistent efforts of restoration pointed to the temple's centrality in their worship of Yahweh. To be sure, the temple was the prescribed point of cultic contact whereby God's presence was manifest in their midst.

Thus when the temple suffered destruction at the hands of foreign invaders, it was an outward sign that God's presence had departed from Israel; similarly, the restoration of the temple was evidence of God's renewed presence and blessing upon Israel.[7] The temple was therefore an indispensable part of Israel's worship. Yet according to the words of Jesus in *St. Mark 13:1–22,* the days of this third temple were also numbered.

In this chapter we will continue to examine human responses that occurred in context with manifestations of God's presence. However, in this chapter our attention will turn to the New Testament period and, more specifically, the person of Jesus Christ. Here, one observes the redemptive-historical shift in the loss of God's dwelling among men, and consider the biblical basis for Christ as God's divine dwelling. Secondly, the biblical data in the Gospels will be examined and discussed as to the theological significance of any human response emerging from connection with the person of Christ.

God's Presence Dwelling in the Person of Jesus Christ

The New Testament presents a distinct shift in the dwelling of God from the temple in Jerusalem to the person of Christ, who himself dwells in his people by the Holy Spirit as the new temple of God's presence. From the vantage point of salvation history, all prior miracles pointed to God's ultimate presence in Jesus Christ. Here, there is a continuous divine *par excellence* where God incarnate dwells among men, in order that he might ultimately dwell within men.

Yet this transition is not initially obvious in the Gospels, since even Christ identified the temple in Jerusalem as *"my Father's house"* (*St .Matthew 21:13, Luke 19:45–46, St. John 2:16–19*), a place where God dwells and a God-ordained site for prayer. The shift becomes more apparent, however, when Christ begins to make remarkable declarations about himself such as, *"I tell you that one greater than the temple is here,"* and *"destroy this temple and I will raise it again in three days"* (*St. Matthew 12:6, St. John 2:19, KJV*). These assertions were scandalous to Jewish ears, for the only thing greater than the temple was God himself; and thus, Christ's declaration was rightly taken as an implicit claim to deity (*St. John 8:58–59; 10:33*).

Additional statements about Christ as God's divine dwelling place appear elsewhere in *St. John 1:14*. The connections of this verse with Christ as God's dwelling are numerous. The first clause declares that the word became flesh and dwelt or tabernacle among us. The verb used in this verse is an aorist indicative form of "to live," or "dwell." A cognate noun also appears in the Old Testament for "Tabernacle" and "tent or meeting place" (*Exodus 25:9; 28:43; 30:16; 33:7–10*) and properly speaking points to one dwelling as in a tent. The place of worship during the wanderings of Israel in the wilderness, the place where God has chosen his presence, was "the Tabernacle," and that noun corresponds to the verb used here. That John wants us to recall God's presence in the tabernacle in the wilderness seems clear from the immediate reference to "glory," for glory was associated with the tabernacle.

The correspondence between the divine encounter of *Exodus 33* and the prologue of *St. John 1* is likewise considerable and further strengthens the contention that *St. John 1:14* has etymological and conceptual ties to the divine appearances in the period of the tabernacle.

Divine transitions were offered when the Samaritan woman raised the issue of whether proper worship to God should take place in the temple or on Mount Gerizim (*St. John 4:20*). *Jesus responded, "Believe me, woman, a time is coming when you will worship the Father neither on this mountain or in Jerusalem. Yet a time is coming when the true worshippers will worship the Father in spirit and truth, for they are the kind of worshippers the Father seeks"* (St. John 4:21–23 KJV).

The One Born of the Spirit

The nature of Christ's birth itself reveals that he was God and Man. Matthew's Gospel tells us that an angel appeared to Joseph in a dream and said, "'Joseph, son of David, do not be afraid to take Mary as your wife; for that which has been conceived in her is of the Holy Spirit. And she will bear a son, and you shall call his name Jesus, for it is he who will save his people from their sins.' Now all this took place to fulfill what was spoken by the Lord through the prophet, 'Behold, the virgin shall be with child, and shall bear a son, and they shall call his name Emmanuel,' which translated means, *"God with us"'* (*St. Matthew 1:20–23*).

In Luke 's account of the birth narrative, the angel answers Mary's question about how this child was to be born to her, a virgin: *"The Holy Spirit will come upon you, and the power of the Most High will overshadow you; and for that reason the holy offspring shall be called the Son of God"* (*St. Luke 1:35, NASB*). Curiously, the virgin birth is never explicitly mentioned elsewhere in the New Testament, but there are several Scriptures that seem to have an awareness of this doctrine:

> *Romans 1:3–4 "the gospel concerning his Son, who was descended from David according to the flesh and designated Son of God in power according to the Spirit of holiness by his resurrection from the dead, Jesus Christ our Lord" (RSV).*

> *Romans 9:5 "Theirs (Israel's) are the patriarchs, and from them is traced the human ancestry of Christ, who is God over all, forever praised! Amen."*

> *Galatians 4:4 "But when the fullness of the time came, God sent forth his Son, born of a Woman, born under the Law, to redeem those under law, that we might receive the full rights of sons. Because*

we are sons, God sent the Spirit of his Son into our hearts, the Spirit who calls out, Abba, Father. So we are no longer a slave, but a son; and a heir."

I Timothy 3:16 "Beyond all question, the mystery of godliness is great: He appeared in a body, was vindicated by the Spirit, was seen by angels, was preached among the nations, was believed on in the world, and was taken up in glory."

The One on Whom the Spirit Remained

A second indication that Christ is the new temple of God's presence among men is found in the testimony of John the Baptist. He declared: *"I have beheld the Spirit descending as a dove out of heaven, and he remained upon him. And I did not recognize him, but he who sent me to baptize in water said to me, 'He upon whom you see the Spirit descending and remaining upon him, this is the one who baptizes in the* Holy Spirit,' And *I have seen, and have born witness that this is the Son of God"* (St. John 1:32–34, NASB).

It remains then, that not only was Christ born of the Sprit, but that the Spirit came upon him in fullness and remained upon him. Thus Jesus would later ask two of his disciples, *"Can you drink the cup I drink or be baptized with the baptism I am baptized with?"* (St. Mark 10:38, KJV). Just as the divine presence rested upon Solomon's Temple in its dedication and consecration in service to God, so also the Spirit's divine presence on Christ marked the beginning of his service and proclamation that, "This time has come. The kingdom of God is near" (*St. Mark 1:15*). Thus a second indication that Christ is the New Testament divine dwelling of God is seen in the fact that he was the one on whom the Spirit came in fullness and remained.

The Attestation of the Divine Presence Voice

The declaration of the Father's love for the Son in *St. John 3:35* demonstrates close correspondence with the baptismal narratives of the synoptic Gospels, where, after the Spirit descended upon Christ, the divine voice of God declared, "You are my Son, whom I love" (*St. Mark 1: 11; St. Matthew 3:17; St. Luke 3:22*). This third indication of Christ as the New Testament divine dwelling of God directly relates to Christ's Sonship and the eternal love relationship between the Father and the Son. This divine presence proclamation is recorded in all three synoptic Gospels,[8] and serves as an attestation that Christ is indeed God's chosen mediator and spokesman. And just as God's divine presence descended on Sinai and validated Moses leadership before all Israel, the events surrounding Christ's baptism by John point to a new mediator in whom God's divine glory resides. John the Baptist therefore declares, *"the reason I came baptizing with water was that he might be revealed to Israel" (St. John 1:31,)*. It was in the waters of John's baptism that the divine voice revealed God's true dwelling place among men.

Human Responses to the Person of Christ

Immediately following Christ's baptism, Scripture describes him as "full of the Holy Spirit" (*St. Luke 4:1*) and, after a period of temptation by Satan in the wilderness (*St. Luke 4:2f),* Christ returned to Galilee "in the power of the Spirit" (*St. Luke 4:14*) to begin his public ministry. It is at this point that the subject of this study takes on particular significance, for here Christ begins to manifest the presence of God in his own person; he forgives sin and demonstrates his authority to do so with physical healings (*St. Mark 2:5–12*) and the casting out of demons, who declare, "what have you to do with us, O Son of God? Have you come to torment us before the time?" *(St. Matthew 8:29*), and hereby proclaims that the "Kingdom of heaven is at hand" (*St. Matthew 3:2*).

The text states with good reason that, "the crowds were astonished at his teaching, for he taught them as one who had authority, and not as their scribes" (*St. Matthew 7:28–29*).

That Christ's own deity among men is largely veiled during his earthly ministry is the particular challenge of treating manifestations of the presence of God in the person of Christ. We see only occasional glimpses of that deity when the glory of who Christ is in and of himself breaks through and affects those around him. On the other occasions, the Holy Spirit's divine presence manifested God's presence through Christ (*Acts 10:38*), or God the Father manifested his presence to Christ and those around him.

Within this context, the major categories of responses to the person of Christ surface. They are fear and worship, instances where individuals fall to the ground, divine judgment in Christ's presence, divine joy, and foreshadowing of human transformation. I will examine these categories and discuss points of theological significance that arise from the scripture observation.

Christ's Presence Resulted in Fear and Worship

At times, Christ's presence resulted in fear and worship, which should not be surprising. A great deal of the divine encounters with Yahweh in the Old Testament engendered the same response. Thus although Christ's own deity remained veiled through most of his public ministry, such responses remind us, among other things, that the New Testament declaration "Jesus Christ is Lord" is equivalent to "Jesus Christ is Yahweh."

At the birth of the Christ child, an angel made an announcement to a group of shepherds, whom Luke describes as being surrounded by the "glory of the Lord." The shepherds "were terribly frightened" by this shining glory (*St. Luke 2:9*). In this instance, God's presence was not manifested in the person of Christ, but manifest by one of the angels. However, the manifestation in connection with Christ's birth forges a link between divine encounters in the Old Testament and those yet to come in Christ.

Many years later, one of the initial encounters between Simon Peter and Jesus caused a similar response in Peter. *St. Luke 5:4–10* describes a miraculous catch of fish for Simon and his companions when they obeyed Jesus' word to cast out their nets (v.6). This manifestation of Christ's divine authority over the natural order so seized Peter's heart that he fell at Jesus' feet exclaiming, "Depart from me, for I am a sinful man, O Lord!" (v.8). As with numerous Old Testament divine appearances, the divine responses bring forth fear.[9] Jesus told Peter that in spite of his fear they will be enjoined together, and he will be part of the ministry catching men instead of fish (v. 10).

Worship is a response to Christ's own deity. In *St. Matthew 14:25–33* Christ approaches his disciples by walking on the sea in the middle of the night. They consider him a phantom, but Christ calms their fear (v. 26–27). Once Jesus steps into the boat, the wind stops (v. 32). The disciples do something demonstrating their perception of Christ's self-revelatory statement (v. 33): "and those who were in the boat worshipped him, saying, 'You are certainly God's Son!'" The fear and superstition of moments before turn to worship and a declaration of Christ's deity as the full implications of Christ's authority over the natural elements take hold. The impact of the Holy Sprit changes the disciples' behavior many times.

That his deity was more often veiled during his earthly ministry explains why instances of dreadful fear and worship overcoming those around him do not occur as in so many Old Testament divine encounters.

Christ's Presence Resulted in Individuals Falling to the Ground

Fear and worship were not the only responses that accompanied manifestations of Christ's divine presence.

There were also occasions where individuals fell to the ground, either voluntarily to worship, voluntarily but in fearful worship, or involuntarily as a result of Christ's divine presence. On at least two occasions, fear and falling occur simultaneously (Peter falling at Jesus knees in *St. Luke 5:8–10* and the disciples' response at Christ's transfiguration in *St. Matthew 17:1–8*).

Voluntarily Falling to Worship or Honor: Some individuals responded to Christ's presence by voluntarily falling to the ground in worship or obeisance. The first recorded act of reverence shown to Christ is found in *St. Matthew 2:2*. With the appearance of the star in the sky, Magi from the east came with the express purpose of worshipping Christ, an intention carried out upon seeing him. "They fell down and worshipped him" (v. 11). Note how many times St. Matthew uses the term worship in the contexts:

> *St. Matthew 2:2 - "Where is he who has been born king of the Jews? For we have seen his star in the East, and have come to worship him" (KJV).*

> *St. Matthew 2:8–"And Herod sent them to Bethlehem, saying, 'Go and search diligently for the child, and when you have found him bring me word, that I too may come and worship him'" (KJV).*

> *St. Matthew 2:11 - "And going into the house they saw the child with Mary his mother, and they fell down and worshipped him. They opened their treasures and offered gifts, gold and frankincense and myrrh" (KJV).*

> *St. Matthew 8:2 - "And behold, a leper came to him and knelt before him, saying, 'Lord, if you will, you can make me clean'" (KJV).*

St. Matthew 9:18 - "While he was thus speaking to them, behold, a ruler came in and knelt before him saying, 'My daughter has just died; but come and lay your hand on her, and she will live"(KJV).

St. Matthew 15:25 - "But the Canaanite woman came and knelt before him, saying, 'Lord, help me *"(KJV).*

St. Matthew 18:26 - "So the servant fell on his knees, imploring him, 'Lord, have mercy on me"(KJV).

The Impact of the Holy Spirit or presence of God moved these leaders to bow down in worship before a Jewish child, who would one day be the Savior of the world. This incident is clearly an end time glimpse of God's ruling and reigning Messiah.

On two separate occasions in Luke's Gospel, lepers approach Jesus for cleansing. The first leper fell on his face requesting to be healed (*St. Luke 5:12*). In this context, the leprous individuals were undoubtedly offering a display of obeisance, but not necessarily worship. However, in *St. Luke 17:11–19,* there is a similar account of Christ cleansing ten lepers. The text describes that one of the ten, upon seeing that he was cleansed, turned back "glorifying God with a loud voice, and he fell on his face at Jesus feet, thanking him" (v. 15–16). In this context, no clear line of demarcation was made between the act of glorifying God with a loud voice and falling on his face at Jesus feet to thank him.

Christ draws the two actions even closer together in a subtle rebuke of the ingratitude of the other nine when he says, "Was no one found who turned back to give glory to God, except this foreigner?" (v.18). Christ makes the implication of the Samaritan's actions very clear in this case. The act of returning to praise God in a loud voice and bow down at his feet to give thanks was deemed *"to give glory to God."* Had such a worshipful response been offered to a man who was simply a vessel of God's manifest presence, the appropriate reply from Jesus would have been the same as Peter's in *Acts 10:26*—"Stand up; I too am just a man." But such is not the case with the Son of God; his reply is simply, "Rise, and go your way; your faith has made you well" (v. 19).

Thus we see that in addition to responses of fear and worship, some individuals voluntarily prostrated themselves in worship and obeisance before the manifest presence of God. Such actions were not only deemed proper and fitting in these contexts, but anything less would be considered a sign of scorn and ingratitude toward God himself. In this way, the actions of these individuals were both complementary and contrary to the cultural standards of the day—it was inconceivable that worship to God could be offered to any man.

Voluntarily Falling in Fearful Worship or Obeisance: In response to manifestations of the divine presence of Christ, other individuals voluntarily fell to the ground, but the motivation for such obeisance before Christ was also laced with fear. Earlier we observed that in *St. Luke 5:8–10,* Peter fell at Jesus' knees crying, "Depart from me, for I am a sinful man, O Lord!" and that Jesus calmed his fear and called him to service. Peter's response to Christ's display is described as "the sense of unworthiness (*St. Matthew 8:8; Job 42:5*) and fear (*Judges 6:22; 13:22; Isaiah 6:5*) which men should feel in the presence of the divine." In this event, it seems to indicate a general sense of moral guilt, a conviction brought about simply by being present during a manifest moment of Christ's divine power.

The Impact of the Holy Spirit brings Joy

As with Yahweh's presence in Old Testament with Israel, Christ's presence also evoked joy among those who were considered his covenantal friends. For the purposes of theological discussion, we shall distinguish the New Testament data on this subject as joy in a present experience, or eschatological joy that is yet to come in Christ's kingdom.

Joy as a Present Experience: If there is one characteristic that marks the coming of the dwelling of God among men in the person of Christ, it is joy. *The angel's declaration at Christ's birth was, "I bring you good news of a great joy which shall be for all the people; for today in the city of David there has been born for you a Savior, who is Christ the Lord"* (*St. Luke 2:10–11 KJV*). Earlier when Mary and Elizabeth met, upon hearing the voice of Mary, Elizabeth's child John leaped in her womb for joy *(St. Luke 1:41–44).* John the Baptist later identified the experience of joy with the person of Christ when he declared: *"He who has the bride is the bridegroom; the friend of the bridegroom who stands and hears him, rejoices greatly at the bridegroom's voice; therefore this joy of mine is now full" (St. John 3:29 KJV).*

Crossing major salvation-historical lines, even Abraham was said to have rejoiced that he was to see Christ's day; he saw it and was glad (*St. John 8:56).* Thus, the very beginning of Christ's dwelling among men was marked by joy and gladness.

Why is joy such an integral part of Christ' presence among men? Joy and gladness is the atmosphere that results from the manifest presence of the God who rejoices. God desires for everyone to receive this joy and be happy. Christ further substantiated these observations when he spoke of God's own joy with these words, *"Just so, I tell you, there will be more joy in heaven over one sinner who repents than over ninety-nine righteous persons who need no repentance"* (*St. Luke 15:7–10 KJV*). Indeed, the link between God's loving nature and the experience of his divine joy are inseparable (*I John 4:8–16*). In *St. John 15:10–12, Jesus says, "If you keep my commandments, you will abide in my love; just as I have kept my Father commandments, and abide in his love. These things I have spoken to you, that my joy may be in you, and that your joy may be full. This is my commandment, that you love one another, just as I have loved you"(KJV).*

Eschatological Joy: Scripture testifies that while Christ was on earth he experienced joy in the Holy Spirit (*St. Luke 10:21*). This expression simply means that Christ experienced joy in the atmosphere of God's presence. The disciples are recorded in several instances as experiencing this divine joy in some measure while they were present with Christ. For example, during the triumphal entry of Christ into Jerusalem, "the whole multitude of the disciples began to praise God joyfully with a loud voice, for all the miracles which they had seen. They began to say, *'Blessed is the King who comes in the name of the Lord; peace in heaven and glory in the highest!'"* (*St. Luke 19:37–38*). Surely such an entry was simply a preview of the glory and joy that will accompany Christ's *parousia* to establish his kingdom over the New Jerusalem.

Likewise, after the resurrection, the disciples "rejoiced when they saw the Lord" (*St. John 20:20*), a rejoicing that continued even after Christ blessed them at his ascension, when they are said to have *"returned to Jerusalem with great joy and were continually in the Temple, praising God"* (*St. Luke 24:50–53*). Divine joy in Christ's presence is certainly a very real and present experience for those who are at covenantal peace with him.

The primary emphasis of Jesus' teaching in this section is on the future blessedness of those who lack in this present world on account of their relationship to Jesus Christ. The theme of God turning weeping into laughter follows after the Old Testament patterns of restoration, whereby God will turn sorrow to joy (*Isaiah 60:20; 61:3*). God wants that true fellowship with man. God desires man to dwell in his presence, but man must yield to the Holy Spirit.

A final human response to God's manifest presence in the person of Christ is seen in instances of bodily transformation, where the corporeal aspect of man's nature is transfigured to image the glory and splendor of God. *I Timothy 3:16 says, "Without controversy, great is the mystery of godliness: God was manifest in the flesh, justified in the*

Spirit, seen of angels, preached unto the Gentiles, believed on in the world, received up into glory" (KJV).

In summary, therefore, the following human responses in connection with manifestations of Christ's divine presence are: (1) fear and worship, (2) a voluntary and involuntary falling to the ground, (3) joy as a present experience and as an eschatological promise.

Theological Significance of Human Responses to Christ's Presence

At the on-set of this chapter, the goals were to first observe the redemptive historical shift in God's dwelling from the tabernacle and temple to the person of Jesus Christ. Second, the biblical data in the Gospels where different human responses occurred in connection with the person of Christ were consulted. The following theological observations emerged as a result of these data.

The Phenomena Point to Christ as True God and True Man

In this chapter, a major shift in God's divine dwelling place from the temple to the person of Christ was observed, but this observation might only indicate that Christ was uniquely blessed with God's divine presence in an unprecedented way. The New Testament, however, went further than assert that Christ is God's unique anointed One; it also declared that he is the eternal and true God (*St. John 1:1*).

Christ's Deity: The strong continuity between various human responses to Yahweh's presence in the Old Testament and responses to Christ's presence in the New Testament communicate Christ's deity. The most significant among these responses included individuals reacting to Christ's presence with intense fear and trembling, a falling to the ground in worship, thanksgiving, and Christ's own foreshadowing of his authority to judge all men in the divine glory of *parousia.* Christ was far more than a prophet or a man, he is our Saviour and Lord. The continuity of these phenomena with the Old Testament text confirm Christ as Yahweh incarnate.

Individuals Respond to Christ's Presence with Fear, Trembling, and Worship

In nearly every Old Testament divine encounter, the individuals present were overcome with a deep sense of fear and trembling at the holiness and majesty of God's presence (*Genesis 3:8; Exodus 3:6; 19:16, 18*). As noted, such responses were caused by recognition of the inherent disharmony that exists between God's holy character and of fallen man's character. God moved on numerous occasions to comfort such fear, His response was, *"Oh, that they had such a heart in them, and that they would fear me, and keep all my commandments always, that it may be well with them and their sons forever!"* (*Deuteronomy 5:29 KJV*). Fear and trembling often accompanied manifestations of Yahweh's presence.

This point of continuity with the OT is also illustrated in instances where people fell before Christ's feet in obeisance and worship. In other New Testament contexts where worship was offered to men who were simply vessels or mediums of God's manifest presence, the recipients refused such veneration, recognizing that worship and reverence of his nature belonged solely to God (*Acts 10:26; 14:11–18; Revelation 22:8–9*). Christ, in contrast, not only received such honor, but also explicitly equated the thanksgiving and worship directed to him as offered to God (*St. Luke 17:18*).

Individuals Fell to the Ground: Another phenomenon that pointed to the continuity between the Old Testament and New Testament responses to Christ's presence was seen in many instances where individuals fell to the ground before Christ. As noted in earlier chapters, there were occasions when individuals fell to the ground in fear and worship or to demonstrate an attitude of submission to God's sovereignty (*Genesis 17:3*).

In the Old Testament, people also fell involuntarily on several occasions when confronted with the majesty of God's presence. *Exodus 33:8–10 says, "And it came to pass, as Moses entered into the tabernacle, the cloudy pillar descended, and stood at the door of the tabernacle, and the Lord talked with Moses. And all the people saw the cloudy pillar standing at the tabernacle door: and all the people rose up and worshipped, every man in his tent door" (KJV)*. The same thing happened to Solomon after he was dedicating the Temple back to the Lord (*II Chronicles 7:1–4*). We observed a similar New Testament response on one rare occasion in *St. John 18:4–9* when the guards were unable to stand before Christ.

For one brief instance, Christ's captors were subject to a manifestation of the glory in his person and, like Moses and Solomon's temple priests before them, they involuntarily fell to the ground. Among other things, this response testifies to the fact that he was the one to be crucified. It served also as a reminder that one day all men will fall to the ground before Christ, some voluntarily for worship and praise, others involuntarily to hear the pronouncement of his sovereign and righteous judgment.

The centerpiece of Christ's ministry is visible in his desire to comfort the human response of fear and trembling in the manifest presence of God, just as Moses had done (*Exodus 20:20*). The words of exhortation were often followed by a declaration of God's good intentions toward the individual in the form of a call to service, words of grace, the forgiveness of sins, or bodily healing (*St. Matthew 14:25–26; 17:2–7*). Particularly notable examples occurred throughout the Gospels when Christ declared an individual's sins were forgiven (*St. Matthew 9:2–7; St. Luke 5:20–26*). The knowledge of peace with God is the beginning to restoration in his joyful presence.

Christ's mission centered on restoring fallen man to the image of his Creator and to receive the true joy of his heart. Christ's divine will for man is to dwell in his presence.

Chapter Five

PENTECOST AND THE GROWTH
OF THE NEW TESTAMENT CHURCH

Introduction

In Christ, God's presence and glory dwelled in fullness among men. *St. John 1:14* says, *"And the Word was made flesh, and dwelt among us, (and we beheld his glory, the glory as of the only begotten of the Father), full of grace and truth"(KJV)*. The disciples had come to know about the Holy Spirit through the life and ministry of Jesus and had even participated in that ministry. They had seen Christ heal the sick and cast out demons or unclean spirits (*St. Matthew 10:1; St. Mark 6:7*). These empowerments were directly mediated by Christ and were strictly intended to serve as an extension of his own Messianic presence. While Christ was on earth, he alone was God's anointed.

In the fourteenth chapter of St. John's Gospel, Christ told his disciples that his presence among them in this age was not permanent, and that after his departure he would not leave them comfortless (v. 18). Rather, the Holy Spirit, "Whom the Father will send in (Christ's) name" (v. 26), will assume a new depth of relationship with the disciples and take up residence within them. The Holy Spirit's indwelling, divine presence will thereby serve to demonstrate three unions to the disciples: 1) Christ's union with the Father, 2) the disciples' union with Christ, and 3) Christ's union with them (v.20). Consequently, God's divine presence will no longer be among his people, but from here forward will be characterized as *within* them.

The aim of this chapter is to examine the varied human responses that occurred in connection with manifestations of God's presence among the people of God in the first century church. Unlike divine encounters with Yahweh in the OT and with the person of Christ in the NT, the majority of passages in this section of the study will center on the Holy Spirit's divine presence as he dwells within the people of God. Other relevant divine passages in the Pauline and general epistles are also of interest as we attempt to sketch a picture of God's final dwelling with man in this closing age. This section concludes with a discussion of the significant theological points that emerge from biblical data.

The Church as
the New Divine Temple of God's Presence

In His post-resurrection appearances, Christ told his disciples, *"Peace be with you; as the Father has sent me, I also send you."* (*St. John 20:21–22*). This motif of the Father sending the Son is one of the master thoughts of John's Gospel (*St. John 3:17, 34; 4:34; 5:23–38, 6:29, 38–57*). It is raised here by Jesus to demonstrate that the commission the disciples were receiving was, in fact, an extension of the same commission He had received.

On the heels of this commission, *St. John 20:22* recorded that *"Christ breathed on his disciples, declaring to them, to receive the Holy Spirit."* Christ's purpose in breathing in this manner seems to signify the beginning of a new creation. Note that it is the same verb used in *Genesis 2:7*—"Then the Lord God formed man of dust from the ground, and breathed into his nostrils the breath of life; and man became a living soul." The term also surfaces in the Greek version of *Ezekiel 37:9,* which states: *"Then he said to me, prophesy to the wind, prophesy, son of man, and say to the wind, thus saith the Lord God; come from the four winds, O breath, and breathe upon these slain, that they may live" (KJV).* Jesus was in essence breathing upon his disciples in anticipation of the bestowal of the Holy Spirit, who would bring about a new creation and empowerment for service in the context of the new covenant.[10]

The scriptures listed below show that the only way that God's divine presence will dwell with man is by having the Holy Spirit: *St. John 3:5–7; 4:24; 6:63; 14:16–26; 15:26–27; 16:7–14, St Luke 1: 41–45; 63–67; 3:16–23; 4:1–18; 24:45–53, Acts 1:4–8; 2:1–4, 38–42; 4:31–32; 8:12–17; 9:15–18; 10:44; 11:15–18; 19:1–6, Romans 8:8–11; 14–27.* The Day of Pentecost was of great significance for these first generation disciples of Christ. Under the old covenant, God only poured out his Spirit upon individuals who were appointed by him to leadership positions (for example—prophets, priests, kings, and judges), or those assigned specific God-ordained tasks. Moses, however, anticipated the blessing of God's presence upon the entire assembly when he responded to Joshua, *"Would that all of Yahweh's people were prophets, that Yahweh would put his Spirit upon them!"* (*Numbers 11:29*). Likewise, Ezekiel and Jeremiah foresaw a time when God would put his Spirit within his people and thereby enable them to keep his laws (*Jeremiah 31:33; Ezekiel 36:27*). As the time for the fulfillment of God's promise drew nearer, Joel foretold more specifically that God would *"Pour out his Spirit upon all flesh; and your sons and daughters shall prophesy, your old men shall dream dreams, your young men shall see visions: And also upon the servants and the handmaids in those days will I pour out my Spirit"* (*Joel 2:28 KJV*).

St. Luke 24:44 records Jesus saying, *"Thus it is written and thus it behooved Christ to suffer, and to rise from the dead the third day: And that repentance and remission of sins should be preached in his name among all nations, beginning at Jerusalem. And ye are witnesses of these things, and behold, I send the promise of my Father upon you: but tarry ye in the city of Jerusalem, until ye be endured with powered on high"* (*KJV*).

After Christ had ascended to heaven, the disciples gathered in Jerusalem in obedience to the Lord's command (*Acts 1:4, 8*). Luke tells us there were about one hundred and twenty in the upper room waiting for the Holy Spirit. Even Mary, the mother of Jesus, was found among those awaiting the arrival of the Holy Spirit. Luke's initial description of this divine event indicates that its origin was from heaven, just as his earlier Gospel narrative describes that the Spirit's descent on Christ was preceded by the observations that "heaven was opened" (*St. Luke 3:21–22*). Notice once again the need for the biblical author to use language of analogy to describe this divine encounter–the noise from heaven was *"like a violent rushing wind"* and *"there appeared to them tongues as of fire which sat upon each of them and they were filled with the Holy Ghost as the Spirit gave them utterance"*(*Acts 2:2–4*).

This language of filling is likewise used metaphorically, expressing in a tangible manner the inward effects of the Spirit's indwelling the disciples. These phenomena, both external and internal, indicate that the new covenant presence of the Spirit had come at last.

The Holy Spirit

The Holy Spirit: The term comes from a Greek word *pneuma,* which is defined as "a breath; a current of air, a breeze, Christ's spirit." It is a cleansing and purifying power. The Holy Spirit is used to designate another manifestation of God, another office as he works and moves in the hearts and lives of men and women. The Holy Spirit is Jesus Christ dwelling within us in the power of his resurrection life. The

Holy Spirit is God flowing forth in blessing, salvation, and power. The Holy Spirit conveys intangibility, incorporeality, immateriality, and personality. The Holy Spirit is not flesh and bones, neither is it a substance. The Holy Spirit represents energy, drive, dynamic movement, and vital force. The Holy Spirit represents sacredness, reverence, purity, righteousness, majesty, and glory.

The Function(s) of the Holy Spirit: In *St. John 4:24,* Jesus told the Samaritan woman, *"God is a Spirit: and they that worship him must worship him in spirit and in truth"(KJV).* The fact that he is a spirit would not be a new revelation to the Jews, nor in all probability to the Samaritans. Worship must be in the spirit and in truth. This can hardly be intelligible if it is not an indirect allusion to *the* Spirit of truth, which would lead the believers in Christ into true worship. In *St. John 16:13–14,* the Spirit is essentially self-effacing, never speaking on his own authority. He does not seek his own glory; only the glory of Christ does it seek. *St. John 15:26* reads, *"But when the Comforter is come, whom I will send unto you from the Father, even the Spirit of truth, which proceeded from the Father, he shall testify of me: And ye also shall bear witness, because ye have been with me from the beginning"* (*KJV*). The Holy Spirit works through the truth, applying it to the hearts of unbelievers in his convicting, convincing work (*St. John 16:8*). The unbeliever must be able to understand what the Spirit is saying. It must go through his mind in order to reach his heart. The impact of the Holy Spirit makes them fall down to repent, worship and honor God.

The Spirit bears witness to Christ, and believers through the same Spirit bear witness to the same Christ. Without the Spirit, the witness to Christ would never have spread. The Spirit helps us to recall and understand his teaching, and guides us into all truth; then we can spread the Gospel (*St. John 14:26, St. John 16:*13). The truth embraces the developing understanding of the meaning of the mission of Jesus and the significance of his death, burial, and resurrection. The Spirit gives our life new faith. The promise of the guidance into all truth accounts for the authority of the epistles. *St. John 16:8* confirms one task of the Holy Spirit. *"The Holy Spirit will reprove the world of sin, and of righteousness, and of judgment: of sin, because they believe not" (KJV).*

Righteousness is defined in relation to Christ; his passion would bring a new dimension to the understanding of righteousness, and would show the world its ignorance of what true righteousness means. Judgment is related to the prince of this world. It is the Spirit's task to show how the forces of darkness have been effectively overthrown. Convictions are the first step in the sinner being saved. The Holy Spirit anoints the Word that is being preached, quickens it to the heart and conscience of the hearer, awakens him to an awareness of his lost condition, and causes him to see himself a sinner. He can never repent until he first experiences the Holy Ghost's conviction of sin. Salvation is the work of the Holy Spirit in the heart of a man from beginning to ending.

The Holy Spirit Regenerates: In *St. John 3:5,* Jesus says, *"Except a man be born of water and of the Spirit, he cannot enter into the kingdom of God" (KJV). Titus 3:5* informs readers that the work of regeneration is the changing of a sinner into a saint, causing a man to become a new creation in Christ Jesus.

The Holy Spirit of God Indwells: In *Romans 8:9,* Paul writes that *"we are not in the flesh, but in the Spirit, if so is that the Spirit of God dwells in you. Now if any man has not the Spirit of Christ, he is none of his" (KJV). I Corinthians 6:19* states, *"Know ye not that your body is the temple of the Holy Ghost which is in you, which ye have of God, and ye are not your own" (KJV).* The Holy Spirit fills the temple and dwells there.

The Holy Spirit Endues With Power: Acts 1:8 states, *"But ye shall receive power, after that the Holy Ghost is come upon you: and ye shall be witnesses unto me both in Jerusalem, and in all Judea, and in Samaria, and unto the uttermost part of the earth" (KJV)*. The word "power," in this instance, comes from the same root as the word "dynamite." This is actually the power of God coming into the life of an individual. It gives him the power to overcome and live victoriously over sin; as well, it gives him power to witness to souls of the saving grace of Jesus. The Holy Spirit gives direction, strength, and empowers us as believers to accomplish the mission.

The Holy Spirit Seals: Ephesians 1:13 and *4:30* inform us to *"grieve not the Holy Spirit of God whereby ye are sealed" (KJV)*. "Sealed" may be defined as exercising ownership, security, and approval to say the work has been completed.

The Character of the Spirit: There are two distinctive titles used in the following passages: *St. John 14:26, 15:26;* and *16:7.* Both convey some aspect of the character of the Holy Spirit. The first is the word *Paraclete,* which is difficult to translate into English. It is variously rendered *Comforter, Advocate, Counselor, or Helper.* Since its root meaning in Greek is "one called alongside," there is no doubt an element of truth in all these suggestions. It should be noted that the word also occurs in *1 John 2:1,* where *"Advocate"* would be the most appropriate translation. The main characteristics conveyed by the name *Paraclete* are more precisely seen in the functions attributed to the Spirit.

The other title, the "Spirit of truth," speaks for itself. Truth is a recurrent theme in the Gospel of John and it is not surprising, therefore, that the Spirit is described as the embodiment of truth. In the prologue, grace and truth are seen to come through Jesus Christ (*St. John 1:17*). The whole message of the Gospel exalts truth above error. The Spirit is therefore seen as the custodian of truth. In these passages of Scripture, there is a close connection between the Spirit and the Word, which may be regarded as an important characteristic of the Gospel. The Spirit shares and communicates the nature of truth. In *St. John 15:26,* the Spirit proceeds from the Father. It informs the reader that the Spirit shares the same nature as the Father. Not only does the Spirit come from God, but the Father also sends him.

The *Paraclete* is seen to be both one with God and at one with man. Another feature is the personal character of the Spirit. This comes out clearly in the variety of functions he performs, many of which would be unintelligible if not regarded as personal. In addition to this, Jesus spoke of another *Paraclete* showing that the *Paraclete* must be as personal as Jesus himself. They are in full agreement. *St. John 14:17* speaks about the *Paraclete* dwelling in the believer forever. This suggests that once the Spirit has taken possession, he remains in residence.

Divine Perfections: The Holy Spirit is omnipresent (*Psalm 139:7*); thus, wherever I go, he is there. He is always present and ever-present. He is omniscient—all seeing, searching all things and knowing all things. He is omnipotent—all-powerful. A simple observation of his handiwork—creation, providence, incarnation, regeneration and sanctification—will attest to his power. The Holy Sprit manifests himself in any manner he chooses. He knows the will of God and makes intercession for the saints with mourning and groaning.

Acts: St. Luke gives us a good view of the Holy Spirit–a foreshadowing of what was to come. The activity of the Spirit is, in fact, in continuity with the mission of Jesus. The Spirit dominates the whole development of ideas in the early history of the Christian movement. For this reason, the evidence in the book of Acts is more historical than didactic, but is nonetheless as important for the special contribution it makes. St. Luke shows that he sees this book as the outcome of revelations of the Spirit from the risen Lord to the apostles (*Acts 1:2*).

The Lord had already communicated with the disciples that he was going to rise on the third day and that repentance and remission of sins should be preached in his name among all nations, beginning at Jerusalem. He even commissioned them as witnesses of these things. Jesus said, *"I would send the promise of my Father upon you: but tarry ye in the city of Jerusalem, until ye are endued with power from on high"* (*St. Luke 24:47–49 KJV*).

In *Acts 1:4–8,* the disciples obey Jesus, and they went to Jerusalem and tarried, waiting for the promise of the Father. This is the same promise that Jesus spoke about in *St. John 14:26, "But the Comforter, which is the Holy Ghost, whom the Father will send in my name, he shall teach you all things, and bring all things to your remembrance, whatsoever I have said unto you"(KJV).*

The Outpouring at Pentecost: Acts 2:1–4 records, *"And when the day of Pentecost was fully come,"* all the disciples and women (which includes Mary the mother of Jesus) *"were all with one accord in one place, and suddenly there came a sound from heaven as of a rushing mighty wind, and it filled all the house where they were sitting, and there appeared unto them cloven tongues like as of fire, and it sat upon each of them, and they were all filled with the Holy Ghost, and began to speak with other tongues, as the Spirit gave them utterance"(KJV).* The accompaniments of the outpouring of the Spirit were symbolic. The wind and fire represented the power of the Spirit, one unseen and the other seen; these extraordinary signs must be regarded as singular to this initial experience since they are not repeated elsewhere. This may also apply to the distinctive manifestation of the Spirit when the apostles began witnessing in tongues.

The symbolic use of wind for Spirit has already been met in *St. John 3:8* and the connection between fire and Spirit ties up with John the Baptist's prediction in *St. Matthew 3:11.* The infilling of the Spirit is extended to all believers. The promise of the Holy Spirit was made to those who repent, are baptized, and receive forgiveness (*Acts 2:38*). This meant all that truly repented, believed, and identified themselves with the existing group of believers would receive the gift of the Spirit. It must be assumed, therefore, that all the 3,000 who were baptized also received the Spirit.

The Spirit was available to all believers. In *Acts 10:44–48,* the manifestation accompanied the initial outpouring of the Holy Spirit on Gentiles; thus, we are shown that God is no respecter of persons.

In his Day of Pentecost message, Peter states (as is recorded in *Acts 2:39*), *"For the promise is unto you, and to your children, and to all that are afar off, even as many as the Lord our God shall call" (KJV).* We must have God's Spirit within us in order to accomplish the mission that God has set before us.

The Pauline Epistles: There are a few statements in these letters that confirm the mighty work of the Spirit in the preaching ministry of the apostle Paul. In *I Corinthians 2:1– 4,* Paul informs the reader that he didn't come with enticing words of man's wisdom, but in demonstration of the Spirit and of power. Paul is concerned that faith should not rest in man's wisdom. This does not mean that Spirit-endowed preaching is opposed to human wisdom; rather, that human wisdom is not the source of the message. According to Paul, the Spirit's task is not simply to draw attention to the glories of the risen Christ, but also to take an essential part in the process of regeneration. Paul's approach is closely related to the teaching in *St. John 3:5* that all believers are possessors of the Spirit. In other words, no one can respond to the claims of Christ without being activated and indwelled by the Holy Spirit.

Paul informs readers that God has given the Spirit to believers (*I Thessalonians 4:8*). There is no distinction between those of the Thessalonians who have and who don't have the Holy Spirit, because God is not a respecter of persons. *I Corinthians 12:13* and *Ephesians 4:4* both lead us to the conclusion, *"that all believers are said to be baptized into one body by one Spirit" (KJV).* The unity brought about by the same Spirit exists across such diverse groups as Jews and Gentiles, slaves and freemen. The most clearly expressed statement in the letters is found in *I Corinthians 12:3;* here Paul says that no one can say *"Jesus is Lord except by the*

Holy Spirit" (KJV). A more general affirmation is found in *Romans 8:9, "Now if any man have not the Spirit of Christ, he is none of his" (KJV)*. It is very clear that the Spirit works to ensure that a Christian knows that he belongs to Christ.

The Spirit is what distinguishes a believer from an unbeliever. In *I Corinthians 3:16* and *6:19,* Paul writes about the Holy Spirit dwelling in our temple, which is the physical body of believers. *"If any man defile the temple of God, him shall God destroy; for the temple of God is holy. Which temple are you? We are bought with a price, the precious blood of Jesus, so we must glorify God in our body, and in our spirit." II Corinthians 1:21–22* states, *"We have been established, anointed and sealed with the Holy Spirit in our hearts."* In *Titus 3:5,* Paul informs us that our righteousness had nothing to do with our salvation; rather, it was the mercy of God, by the washing of regeneration and renewing of the Holy Ghost. In *Hebrews 2:4,* Paul writes that *"God also bear them witness, both with signs and wonders, and with various miracles, and gifts of the Holy Ghost, according to his own will."*

The Petrine Epistles are in line with the mainstream New Testament documents in assuming a high doctrine of the Spirit's activity. It might also be noted in the epistle of Jude that believers possess the Spirit, for the scoffers are denoted by their lack of the Spirit. The believers are encouraged to build up their most holy faith by praying in the Holy Ghost.

God's Presence Now Dwells Within His People

This first observation is a recognition that the faith union that joins new covenant believers together with Christ constitutes what Scripture describes as a spiritual body. Colossians 2:9–10 says, *"For in him dwells all the fullness of the Godhead bodily. And you are complete in him, which is the head of all principality and power" (KJV)*. This new covenant reality is communicated in a variety of ways in the New Testament, each demonstrating a different facet of this glorious union. One of the primary ways is through metaphor. The apostle Paul instructs the Corinthian believers that the entire assembly is "God's Temple where God's Spirit lives" (*I Corinthians 3:16*).[11] This is a metaphor Paul uses elsewhere for the church on only two other occasions. Later on in this letter, Paul warns or admonishes Corinthian believers to flee from sexual immorality. The Christian believer's body is a member of Christ himself (1 Corinthians 6:15), or the temple of the Holy Spirit. Thus, for Paul, union with Christ constitutes oneness with him in Spirit.

This divine coming of the Spirit to God's people is so crucial to the believers that Paul wrote, *"For we were all baptized by one Spirit into one body, whether Jews or Greeks, slave or free and we were all given one Spirit to drink"* (*I Corinthians 12:13*).

The Holy Spirit in the Life of Believers: Sanctification is the overall process by which new believers move toward a life of holiness. Sanctification is governed by its close association with the word "acceptable." The standard of sanctification is holiness that is acceptable to God; that is, holiness in line with the Spirit's own character. Sanctification also means to be set aside for a certain use.

Adoption is used to describe the new relationship into which believers have entered. In *Romans 8:14,* Paul writes, *"All who are led by the Spirit of God are sons of God,"* and *"we cry, Abba, Father."* It is the Spirit himself bearing witness with our spirit that we are the children of God. It is his constant work to remind us of the new family into which we have been adopted. It is one thing to know we are children of God, it is another to act like children of God; this encompasses developing a full awareness of utter dependence on and love for God as Father.

The Holy Spirit also gives liberty. Galatians 5:1–16 says, *"Stand fast therefore in the liberty wherewith Christ hath made you free, and be not entangled again with the yoke of bondage. This I say then, Walk in the Spirit, and ye shall not fulfill the lust of the flesh, for the flesh lusted against the Spirit, and the Spirit against the flesh: and these are contrary the one to the other: so that ye cannot do things that ye would" (KJV).* Paul writes in *II Corinthians 3:17, "Now the Lord is that Spirit: and where the Spirit of the Lord is, there is liberty" (KJV).*

The apostle Paul reminds all spirit-filled believers how they should live in *chapters 3 and 4 of Colossians.* The apostle Paul wrote the book of Colossians to the church at Colosse when he was a prisoner at Rome. He wrote this epistle to warn the Church of the danger of certain unspecified heresies. He professes a great satisfaction in their steadfastness and constancy. Colosse was a city of Phrygia in Asia Minor. The Church at Colosse, a city in the rich Lycus valley east of Ephesus, grew up as a result of Paul's three years of ministry in the province of Asia. Paul never visited this church, though he was acquainted with its leaders and had a very vital interest in its welfare and progress. While Paul was in prison at Rome, he learned of the false teachings that were being propagated in the churches of the province of Asia. The churches at Colosse and Ephesus seem to have been deeply affected by these false teachings.

Paul's job was to preach the Gospel to the Gentiles. There was a flourishing church at Colosse; they were as dear to Paul as the Philippians or any others that were converted by Paul's preaching. Paul tells the saints at Colosse to be good Christians; they must abandon the old ways and adopt the new. The old must be put off, and the new put on. You have died with Christ; thus, you must now act, speak and think in a new manner. The believer is dead to the world and liberated from sin.

Paul explains that though one is made free from the ceremonial law, it does not give one privilege to live any way they want. The Christian must walk closely with God. According to *Colossians 3:1–4, "If you then have risen with Christ, seek those things which are above, where Christ sitteth on the right hand of God. Set your affection, feelings, and mind on things that are above, not on things that are on* the earth. *For you are dead, and your life is hid with Christ in God" (KJV)*. In *Colossians 3:5–11,* Paul says, *"Mortify therefore your members which are upon this earth."* These members include, but are not limited to, "fornication, uncleanness, inordinate affection, evil concupiscence, covetousness, which is idolatry, anger, wrath, malice, blasphemy, filthy communication out of your mouth, and lie not one to another."

Fornication, which appears first in the list of sins, receives the same preeminence among the works of the flesh in *Galatians 5:19–21.* It means primarily traffic with harlots; it includes adultery and incest. It is known as unlawful lust and is found also as a near technical term for any sexual relations outside a marital covenant. More widely, it represents sexual irregularity in general. It is common in Greek/ Roman antiquity. In *I Corinthians 6:18,* Paul says, *"Flee fornication, every sin that a man does is without the body; but he that committed fornication sins against his own body" (KJV).*

Uncleanness means impurity. It includes the misuse of sex, but is applicable to various forms of moral evil. *Inordinate affection* means uncontrolled passion, or lusting, and homosexual behavior. *Evil concupiscence* means unholy desires and all greed. *Covetousness* is spiritual idolatry; it is the giving of that love and regard to worldly wealth, which are due to God only. In the book of *Galatians 5:19,* Paul tell us "to walk in the Spirit, and we shall not fulfill the lust of the flesh. *Galatians 5:19–21* says, *"Now the works of the flesh are manifest, which are these; adultery (sexual vice involving marriage), fornication (unlawful sexual lust), uncleanness (impure/not clean), lasciviousness (lusting), idolatry (image worshipping), witchcraft (magic and drugs/sorcery/ a druggist/magician), hatred (dislike), variance (contention/ debate/strife/quarrel), emulations (jealousy/malice/envy), wrath (fierceness/temper/quick to get mad), strife (contention/quarrels), seditions (division), heresies (disunion/factions), envying/, murders(to kill/tear down), drunkenness (intoxicant), reveling (riotous living).* We must also put away anger, wrath, malice, blasphemy, filthy communication out of your mouth, and don't lie one to another, seeing that we have put off the deeds of the flesh. Lying makes us like the devil, who is the father of lies (*St. John 8:44*). Anger and wrath are bad, but malice is worse. Anger heightens and settles in us, which allows the tongue to speak and boast great things against God and man. In *Ephesians 6:4,26* Paul says, *"Be ye angry, and sin not: let not the sun go down on your wrath."* One is reminded by Paul how to live a Christian life in *Ephesians 5:1,2.* In this passage, he says, *"Be ye followers of God, as dear children; and walk in love, as Christ have loved us, and have given himself for us an offering and a sacrifice to God for a sweet-smelling savior" (KJV).*

Christians must be imitators of God. They must be holy, as God is holy; merciful, as God is merciful; perfect, as God is perfect. Be imitators of God, especially in his love, as dear children, who want to be greatly beloved by their parents. Children are obliged to imitate their parents in what is good. The character that one bears obliges him/her to resemble that of Christ Jesus. Those only are God's children who imitate him and walk in his love. It should be the principle from how we act; it should direct the ends at which we aim. We are all sharers in that love and therefore should love one another. Christ loved us so much that he gave himself for us, and we should do the same in our living.

In *Colossians 3:12–15,* Paul informs the church what to put on after having taken the old man off. *"That those who have put off the old man, have put off the deeds of it, and those who have put on the new man, have put on the deeds, renewed in knowledge" (KJV).* An ignorant soul cannot be a good soul. Light is the first thing in the new creation, as it was in the beginning when God spoke it into existence. It is the believer's duty to put on plenty of mercy and be holy. We must show love to the miserable and have mercy on one another. Be kind always, because the Gospel is to soften the minds of men and also to sweeten them and promote friendship among men, as well as reconciliation with God. *Humbleness of Mind*—there must not only be a humble demeanor, but a humble mind. *Meekness*—prudently bridles our own anger and patiently bears the anger of others.

Long-suffering—many can bear short provocations that are weary of bearing when it grows long. If God is long-suffering to us, we should exercise it to others. *Mutual forbearance/Forbearing one another*—we all have something that needs to be borne with. *Forgiving one another*—Quarrels will sometimes happen, even among the elect of God, who are holy and beloved. It is our duty to forgive one another. Jesus said in *St. Mark 11: 24–26, "Therefore I say unto you, what things so ever ye desire, when ye pray, believe that ye receive them, and ye shall have them. And when ye stand praying, forgive, if ye ought against any: that your Father also which is in heaven may forgive you your trespasses. But if ye do not forgive, neither will your Father which is in heaven forgive your trespasses" (KJV).*

In St. Matthew's Gospel, the disciples asked Jesus how many times they should forgive. Jesus said not merely seven times, but seventy times seven. This has often been interpreted to mean that just as long as your brother sins against you, you should forgive him. There is no limit *(St. Matthew 18:21–22)*.

We must clothe ourselves with *love,* which is the bond of perfection. Jesus laid the foundation in faith, and the top stone is love. Christian unity consists of unanimity and mutual love. We should always let the peace of God rule or govern in our hearts. The peace of God needs to take control of our lives. Being united in one body, we are called to be at peace one with another and to be thankful. The works of thanksgiving to God is such a sweet and pleasant work, that it will help make us sweet and pleasant toward all men. Christ must dwell in us richly; he must keep our house, not as a servant, but as a master.

God's Presence brings Peace unto his People: The response that repeatedly arose in the divine contexts of the

Old Testament pointed to a disharmony, or no peace, between God's holy presence and fallen man. This discord was often evidenced by sin that brought forth human fear, trembling, and fleeing from God's presence.

In the context of the new covenant, the reconciling ministry of Christ changed the responses of sinful man to manifestations of God's presence. The author informs Christians about the heavenly joy and blessings of the new covenant. The Christian believer has come to Jesus, the mediator of a new covenant, and to the sprinkled blood, which speaks better than the blood of bulls and goats. Here one sees that there has not only been a significant change of covenant, but a resultant, fundamental change in man's ability to relate to God's divine presence.

But what precisely has brought about this harmony between God's divine presence and his people? Under the new covenant, God accomplished a positional or forensic change of relationship for the believer through a faith union with Christ. Moreover, the indwelling presence of the promised Holy Spirit is the instrumental means for bringing about a material change in the heart of the believer. The apostle Paul also wrote *Romans 8:3–4, "For what the law could not do, weak as it was through the flesh, God did: sending his own Son in the likeness of sinful flesh and as an offering for sin, he condemned sin in the flesh, in order that the requirement of the Law might be fulfilled in us, who do not walk according to the flesh, but according to the Spirit" (KJV).*

The Holy Spirit Results in a Godlike Atmosphere for Christians Families

Submission is the duty of the whole Christian family. It is agreeable to the order of nature and the reason of things, as well as the appointment and will of God. It is submission as the part of husband and wife, who stand in the nearest relation and are under strict engagements to proper duty. Husbands must love their wives and not be bitter against them. They must love them with tender and faithful affection, as Christ loved the church; they must be kind and obliging to them in all things. In *I Corinthians 7:3,* Paul says, *"Let the husband render unto the wife due benevolence: and likewise also the wife to the husband. The wife has not power over her body, but the husband: and likewise also the husband has not power over his body, but the wife, so defraud ye not one another, except it be with consent for a time, that you may give yourselves to fasting and prayer; and come together again that Satan tempt you not for your incontinence"(KJV).*

The Scripture, in *I Peter 3:1–9,* says, *"Likewise, ye wives, be in subjection to your own husbands; that if any obey not the word, they also may without the word be won by the conversation of the wives. Husbands dwell with them according to knowledge, giving honor unto the wife, as unto the weaker vessel, and as being heirs together of the grace of life; that your prayers be not hindered" (KJV).* Wives being in subjection would be the most likely way to win those unbelieving husbands who had rejected the word, or who attended to no other evidence of the truth than what they saw in the conduct of their wives.

Peter directs Christian wives not to put so much emphasis on excellent and beautiful ornaments, which is the outward adorning; but rather, to "focus on the hidden man of the heart, in which is not corruptible, but a meek and quiet spirit, which is in the sight of God of great price." Take care to adorn and beautify your souls rather than your bodies. The ornaments of the body perish in the using; but the grace of God, the longer we wear it, the brighter and better it is. The finest ornament of Christian women is a meek and quiet spirit. If the husband was harsh, and averse to religion, there is no way so likely to win him as a prudent, meek behavior. A true Christian's chief care lies in the right ordering and commanding of his or her own spirit. The endowments of the inner man are the chief ornaments of a Christian; but especially a composed, calm, and quiet spirit–that makes a man or woman beautiful and lovely.

Ephesians 6:1–4 says, *"Children, obey your parents in the Lord: for this is right. Honour your father and mother; which is the first commandment with promise; that it may be well with you, and you may live long on the earth. And you fathers, provoke not your children to wrath: but bring them up in the nuture and admonition of the Lord" (KJV).* They must be willing to do all the lawful commands, as those who have natural right and are more fit to direct them than themselves. Parents must be tender, and children must be obedient. Let not your authority over them be exercised with rigorous and severity but with kindness and gentleness. Servants, obey your masters in all things according to the flesh. Servants must do the duty of the relation in which they stand in all things, not only when their master's eye is upon them. The fear of God ruling in their heart will make people good in every relation. Whatsoever you do, do it heartily and with diligence, not idly and slothfully but to the Lord and not men. We are really doing our duty to the Lord when we are not slothful, but faithful in our duty to men. We must serve our masters according to the command of Christ.

Christ will avenge you of the masters who mistreat you. He who does wrong will receive for the wrong that he has done. Christ will be sure to punish the unjust as well reward the faithful servant. Paul even addresses slaves. This is evidenced by the letter written to Philemon to illuminate the mutual responsibilities of slaves and masters within the Christian fellowship. It also expresses the transforming effect of this fellowship on their relationship. The relationship belongs to this present world order. In the higher and abiding relationship with Christ, believing slaves and masters are brothers. The slave/master relationship might persist in the home and business life: within the church it was swallowed up in the new relationship. Paul treats the distinction in status between slave and the free person as irrelevant in the new order. He sees the advantage of being free rather than enslaved, and the slave who has an opportunity of gaining freedom is encouraged to make use of the opportunity.

For he who was called in the Lord as a slave is a freedman of the Lord; likewise he who was free when called is a slave of Christ. If a Christian slave had an unbelieving master, he would serve him more faithfully now because the reputation of Christ and Christianity were bound up with the quality of his service. Christian servants should work eagerly and zestfully for a master who was harsh, unconscionable, and ungrateful; for they would receive their thanks not from their master, but from Christ. The Christian servant can work for Christ by serving an earthly master in such a way as to adorn the doctrine of God our Savior in everything. How happy would the Gospel religion make the world if it prevailed everywhere? And how much would it influence every state of things and every relation of life? Our souls prosper when the Word of God lives in us richly.

In *Romans 6:5–18,* Paul reminds us, *"We have been planted together in the likeness of Jesus' death: that like as Christ was raised up from the dead by the glory of the Father, even so we also should walk in newness of life" (KJV).* Christians should not yield their members as instruments of unrighteousness unto sin: but, rather, we should yield our members as instruments of righteousness unto God. Christians are to walk in newness of life, and it brings forth newness of heart. Christians must walk by the Spirit of Christ, make new choices, and choose new paths to walk in and new companions with which to walk.

In *St. Matthew 5:13–16,* Jesus says, *"Ye are the salt of the earth: but if the salt have lost his savor, wherewith shall it be salted? It is good for nothing, but to be cast out, and to be trodden under foot of men. Ye are the lights of the world. A city that is set on a hill cannot be hid. Neither do men light a candle, and put it under a bushel, but on a candlestick; nor it gives light unto all that are in the house. Let your light so shine before men, that they may see your good works, and glorify your Father which is in heaven"(KJV).*

Christians have been justified and sanctified by God. Justification means to have been "uprighted" by God. It transfers the believer into the new age of redemption with Christ. We live under the reign of grace and look confidently to that outcome of eternal life. Christ paid the price for us with his precious blood. It is for the glory of his justice and righteousness. In *Romans 4:7–8,* we read, *"Blessed are they whose iniquities are forgiven and covered. Blessed is the man to whom the Lord will not impute sin."* It is God's not imputing sin that makes it wholly a gracious act of God. God pardoned us and called us blessed people. In *Romans 5:1–2,* Paul reminds us that we, as Christians, must not forget that, *"Being justified,"* (made right) *"by faith, we have peace with God through our Lord Jesus Christ: by whom also we have access by faith into his grace wherein we stand, and rejoice in hope of the glory of God."* God designed our salvation for glory and happiness; he decreed that holiness is the only way. He loves us so; even to the degree that he calls us his friends and made us in his image. God requires his friends (the saints) to be holy, stay holy, and live holy everyday.

All who are made righteous in the sight of God are made holy by the grace of God. *"God loves the Church so much that he gave himself for it; that he might sanctify and cleanse it"* (*Ephesians 5:25–26 KJV*).

In *Colossians 3:1–4,* Paul says, *"If you then be risen with Christ, seek those things which are above, where Christ sits on the right hand of God. Set your affection on things above, not on things on the earth. For you are dead, and your life is hid with Christ in God. When Christ, who is our life, shall appear, then shall you also appear with him in glory"* (*KJV*). The new man has his livelihood, and it is hidden with Christ: not hidden from us only, in point of secrecy, but hidden for us, denoting security. This is our comfort, that our life is hidden with him. It will be his glory to have his redeemed with him, and it will be their glory to come with him. Our head is there, our home is there, our treasure is there, and we hope to be there forever.

In addition to the absence of an inherent disharmony between God's presence and his people under the new covenant, the divine presence of the Spirit also results in a Godlike atmosphere among Christian families and all believers. In one sense, the phenomena that results from this atmosphere are not strictly human in nature, and therefore, may be viewed as outside the scope of this study. However, because of the human responses that often surface in the context of this atmosphere, a brief discussion is warranted.

As mentioned earlier, an important work of the divine Spirit in the life of the believer is to bring about a material change in the character of one's heart and mind that, theologically, is identified with sanctification and is also evident in the communities.

Divine Glory and Sanctification: This relationship is explicit in the following passage where Paul writes to the Corinthians: *"Now the Lord is the Spirit; and where the Spirit of the Lord is, there is liberty. And we, who with unveiled face all reflect the glory of the Lord, are being transformed into the same image from glory to glory" (II Corinthians 3:17–18 KJV).* The Lord, whom Paul describes in verse 16 as taking away the veil that blinds the minds of unbelievers, is also described as the Spirit. In a culminating expression of the antithesis between the old and new covenants, Paul states, "And where the Spirit of the Lord is, there is liberty." It is the new covenant that empowers individuals to turn to the Lord (3:16), whereby the Spirit of the Lord brings liberty through the lifting of the veil that covers the heart and mind (3:14–15). The new covenant, therefore, is a covenant of life and liberty through the divine presence of the Spirit. Paul goes on and describes the believer's new divine relationship to the Spirit in terms that are progressive and cumulative.

The Christian believer, therefore, images an ever-increasing divine glory through the indwelling presence of the Spirit that will one day be culminated in full bodily glorification at the eschaton. For this reason, Paul wrote: *"I consider that our present sufferings are not worth comparing with the glory that will be revealed in us, but we ourselves, who have the first fruits of the Spirit groan inwardly as we await our adoption as sons, the redemption of our bodies" (Romans 8:18, 23 KJV).*

This new divine dwelling of God with men has resulted in God residing within his people rather than just among them. On the basis of Christ's atoning sacrifice and the believer's new standing with God, there is no longer an inherent disharmony between God's presence and his people. The outpouring of the Holy Spirit has had such an impact on man that his relationship with God is restored. The divine presence of the Spirit has also resulted in a God-like atmosphere among the people of God. The great impact of the Holy Spirit upon the lives of believers has transformed them back into the image of God.

Chapter Six

CONCLUSIONS

The Impact of God's Presence
on Mortal Man as a Whole Person

This conclusion recognizes that the human responses we observed throughout this study were just the "tip of the iceberg," of the impact of God's manifest presence on the mortal man; beneath the surface of every outward human response lay a host of emotional and spiritual effects.

Even though Adam and Eve disobeyed God, ran and hid themselves because of sin, and fell out of his divine will, God still loved them (Genesis 3). God dressed them up with the best of clothes, but they still had to pay for their sin. When the children of Israel trembled in Yahweh's presence (*Exodus 19:16*), it was because they feared him and needed a sanctifying heart (*Exodus 20:18*). Likewise, when God later manifested his presence in fire during the period of the tabernacle and the temple (*Leviticus 9:22–24*), the Israelites not only fell with their faces to the ground—thereby showing their inward attitude of fearful reverence—but also burst forth in joyful shouting (v.24). The components of reverential fear, wonder, and awe simultaneously combined with joy in one inward response.

Consequently, the people manifested their emotion in a series of corresponding human actions, each initiated by the inner stirrings of the human spirit in God's presence. The indissoluble connection between the workings of the inner person and corresponding outward behavior needed to be recognized.

Christians must bear in mind that the constituent aspects that make up man's being are interconnected at a fundamental level. We see in *Exodus 20:20* that Moses responds to the people's fear and trembling: "Do not be afraid. God has come to test you, so that the fear of God will be with you to keep you from sinning." A similar sanctifying fear was instilled in the early Christian community with the divine judgment against Ananias and Sapphira (*Acts 5:1–11*). God has given us his Holy Spirit so that we can remain in his presence until he comes. The presence of God—his divine Spirit—also produces a Godlike atmosphere, which brings forth joy and inspired songs of praise and thanksgiving among the people of God (*Ephesians 5:18–20*). These responses sanctify God's people and draw their hearts from illegitimate affections to a pure love for God and his people.

Consequently, man's interaction with the spiritual world may affect his humanity, just as his interaction with the physical world may affect him spiritually. Man must remember that he was created in the image and likeness of God. The process of salvation whereby God restores his image in man is intended to bring man back to the place where he responds to God's manifest presence with every aspect of his being. Therefore, this restoration and sanctification are considered incomplete until the resurrection and glorification of the physical body at the coming of Christ (*St. Luke 21:28; Romans 8:23; Ephesians 4:30; I Corinthians 15:50; Revelation 6:9–11*).

God Desires the Response of the Whole Mortal Man

We might well ask why God affects individuals on a human level at all. Is he not capable of accomplishing his divine purposes in man quietly and unobtrusively on a spiritual level? The answer is yes. But on many occasions in redemptive history, God draws near to individuals, resulting, among other things, in strong human responses. Since these responses are distributed across both Old Testament and New Testament texts, with final culmination occurring only in the eschaton, there is no basis for assuming that such occurrences have ceased in the life of the contemporary church. To be sure, during times of renewal when God draws near to individuals, an understanding of God's purposes in these responses would better equip the church to pastor and guide such phenomena.

Although a full answer to this question of why God at times intends such human responses is beyond the scope and application of this study, the following points do help to bring the issue into a somewhat sharper focus:

At times, God's presence is simply the indirect cause of certain human responses. In the period of biblical history prior to Sinai, many people fell to the ground in Yahweh's presence (*Genesis 17:3; Leviticus 9:24; Deuteronomy 9:18, 25*). Although these responses were clearly occasioned by instances of God's manifest presence, they occurred voluntarily as a willful expression of honor to God himself. In this sense, God was an indirect cause of what was essentially a volitional human response. In contemporary settings, similar responses to God's presence undoubtedly occur. Throughout life, people carry with them different temperaments, upbringings, grieves, and hurts, as well as a host of cultural and religious traditions. Consequently, when God draws near to them there may be voluntary or involuntary human responses that emerge directly from these factors. Are such phenomena rightly called "responses" to God's presence? God's presence is simply a catalyst for what are essentially human reactions that vary from individual to individual. Such responses reflect more about the person than about God.

(2) In many of the instances where God's presence affected individual humans, it is clear that one of God's aims was to influence the total person and receive a total response from that individual in return. For example, at Sinai, God manifested his glory and majesty to the Israelites to such an extent that not only did the mountain tremble (*Exodus 19:18*), but the people trembled in fear of death (*Exodus 20:18; Deuteronomy 5:23–27*). Moses said, *"Do not fear: For God has come to prove you, and that the fear of him may be before your eyes, that you may not sin. I have heard the words of this people, which they have spoken to you; they have rightly said all that they have spoken. Oh that they had such a mind as this always, to fear me and to keep all my commandments, that it might go well with them and with their children for ever"(Deuteronomy 5:28–30 KJV).*

God thereby affected the people at every level of their being so that a deep awareness of who he was would result in a deep and wholehearted attitude toward His holiness, sin, and obedience.

A similar response of the whole person or mortal man is also evident in Daniel chapter 10, where we observe such overwhelming experiences as trembling, falling to the ground, and an inability to breathe in God's presence (*Daniel 10:7*). It is surely significant that God restored Daniel's strength and enabled the prophet to stand once again before addressing him at length by honoring his image in man. But the experience had literally shaken Daniel in his whole being, thus preparing the prophet to receive the Word of the Lord in deep earnest.

Furthermore, even in instances where God's presence resulted in manifestations of joy and blessings, the divine intent often included a response of the mortal man or whole person in such experiences as dancing (*II Samuel 6:14–15; Psalms 30:11; 150:4*), laughter (*Job 8:21; Psalms*

126:2), as well as loud praises and singing (*Psalms 5:11; 27:6; 28:7; 32:11; 81:1; Acts 2:11; Ephesians 5:18–20*).

Paul reminds us in *I Corinthians 15:22, "For as in Adam all die, even so in Christ shall all be made alive." The first man, Adam, was made a living soul; the last Adam, Christ, was made a quickening spirit" (I Corinthians 15:45–47 (KJV)*. David reminds us in *Psalms 51:1–5, "Behold I was shapen in iniquity; and in sin did my mother conceive me."* Paul let us know why we are to be impacted by the Holy Spirit; he says, *"For that which I do, I do not; for what I would, that do I not; but what I hate, that do I. If then I do that which I would not, I consent unto the law that it is good. Now then it is no more I that do it, but sin that dwelleth in me. For I know that in me (that is in my flesh,) dwelled no good thing: for to will is present with me; but how to perform that which is good I find not" (Romans 7:14–18 KJV)*. Paul is reminding us that we must have the impact of the Holy Spirit to deal with this flesh. The only way we can worship God is in *spirit and truth* (*St. John 4:24*), and if we don't have the *Holy Spirit, we are none of his* (*Romans 8:9*). God's intentions in impacting or affecting individual humans indicate his desire for men and women to yield and respond to him with their whole being. God desires the response of the whole person to him. *Nothing less will do.*

AUTOBIOGRAPHY

This world has become infiltrated with trouble, hardship, hurts, and pains. Because of these things, it has become evident that the Spirit of God is a must-have. Without the Holy Spirit, we are helpless. This book reaches to identify the necessity and the impact of the Holy Spirit in the lives of all mankind. The very existence of mankind is dependent on God's Spirit. This book is based solely on the Word of God. Because of this, it is, without a doubt, relevant to every living being, in every country of every continent. This is an excellent book that will enlighten your mind and reveal the power that God has made available to all those who will believe. It is our prayer that you will be endowed with the life-changing power of the Holy Spirit even through your reading of this book. It is also our desire that this book will touch the hearts of men and women all over the world, especially those who have not yet experienced the power of the Holy Spirit in their lives. Your life will never be the same. May God bless you as you read.

Dr. Joe R. Williams Sr. is the Founder and Pastor of the True Love Apostolic Faith Church in Lawton, Oklahoma. Before assuming this position, Dr. Williams was a member of the United States Army. Upon retirement from military service, he worked as a counselor within the Lawton Public

School System. He has endeavored to use his life as a tool in ministering to people of all ages, backgrounds, and nationalities. Dr. Williams has received his Doctorate degree in Ministry (DMN) from American Christian Seminary. Currently, Dr. Williams also serves as a professor with the True Love Bible Institute (an extension of the Aenon Bible College, Indianapolis, Indiana). With all of these accomplishments, Dr. Williams has not failed to remain a devoted husband and father. For 29 years, Dr. Williams has been married to Treddie Jean Williams. He has six children, three daughters-in-law, one son-in-law, and six grandchildren. Also, Dr. Williams has fathered numerous individuals in the Gospel.

ENDNOTES

[1] I Kings 8:10–12, where a cloud filled the earthly temple so that the priests could not perform their services (cf. Exodus 40:34–35 with the tabernacle in the desert), Rev 15:8, where the heavenly temple filled with smoke from the glory of God and no one enter the Temple. In Exodus 19:16; 20: 18–21, God manifests his presence at Sinai, and the people trembled in fear. Clearly, there are theological implications present as these phenomena are recorded and repeated throughout the folds of redemptive history.

[2] The Scripture does not describe one set pattern of human responses that attend the manifestation of God's presence. However, this is not implying that one cannot ultimately determine what Scripture teaches regarding the significance of human responses. Indeed, determining such is the goal of this study.

[3] Notice that the New Testament rejects any conception of "spiritual" faith that does not manifest itself in bodily works: i.e., words spoken, deeds performed, or action refrained from. This is also an implicit testimony to the essential unity in the human constitution (James 2:14–26).

[4] CF. Exodus 33:14, where God declared to Moses: My presence will go with you, and I will give you rest.

[5] *Psalm 34:8*- "Oh taste and see that the Lord is good."

Isaiah 55:1–3- "Come, all you who are thirsty, come to the waters; and you who have no money, come,

Buy and eat! Come, buy wine and milk without money and without cost. Listen, listen to me, and eat

What is good, and your soul will delight in the richest of fare."

St. John 6:51- " I'm the living bread that came down from heaven. If anyone eats of this bread, he will Live forever."

Revelation 2:7- " To him who overcomes, I will give the right to eat from the tree of life, which is in the Paradise of God."

Revelation 2:17- "To him overcomes, I will give some of the hidden manna."

[6] Judges 3:9–11–The spirit of God came upon Othniel, he became a force of God, and he judged Israel and the land rested for forty years.

Judges 6:34–The spirit of God came upon Gideon and he built an altar.

I Samuel 10:10- The spirit of the Lord changed the behavior of Saul.

I Samuel 19:20–24- Saul sent servant out to get David but the sprit fell upon them and they began to prophesize. The spirit of God will change your behavior.

[7] St. Matthew 23:38; St. Mark 13:2 relates to the Temple as the center of Israel's life and the symbol of God's relation to the nations; the broken relationship to God occasions a rejection of the place that served as to the nation; the broken relationship to God occasions a rejection to the place that served as the invisible embodiment of God pleasures, and so a judgment on the nation itself.

[8] Note that John's gospel records an instance of this divine voice when Jesus prayed, "Father, glorify thy name." Then a voice came from heaven, "I have glorified it, and I will glorify it again."

[9] Genesis 15:1; 26:24; Exodus 20:20; Judges 6:23; Daniel 10:12, 19.

[10] There is no reason why St. John 7:39; 16:7; 20:22 must be understood as the actual bestowal of the Spirit promised by Jesus earlier in John's gospel. In defense of this position, we see Jesus tell his disciples in John 16:7, "But I tell you the truth: It is for your good that I go away. Unless I go away, the Holy Spirit, the Counselor, will not come to you; but if I go away, I will send him to you." Here we have an explicit statement that the promise of the Holy Spirit is predicated on Christ's physical absence from the disciples. Also, Acts 1:4 is another imperative statement, which states, "they should not depart from Jerusalem, but wait for the promise of the Father, which is the Holy Spirit. But ye shall receive power, after that the Holy Ghost is come upon you: and ye shall be witnesses unto me both in Jerusalem and in all Judea, and in Samaria, and unto the uttermost part of the earth" (KJV). The reference at the end of Acts 1:4 was actually

fulfilled in Acts 2, not John 20:22. Acts 2:1–4 says, "And when the day of Pentecost was fully come, they were all with one accord in one place. And suddenly there came a sound from heaven as of a rushing mighty wind, and it filled the entire house where they were sitting. And there appeared unto them cloven tongues like as of fire, and it sat upon each of them. And they were all filled with the Holy Ghost, and began to speak with other tongues, as the Spirit gave them utterance."

[11] Paul intends the readers to understand the whole Assembly of God's people in Corinth as the temple of God.

"We are the temple of the living God" (2 Corinthians 6:16); and "In him the whole building (of believers) is joined together and rises to become a holy temple in the Lord." (Ephesians 2:21).

TATE PUBLISHING, LLC

Tate Publishing is committed to excellence in the publishing industry. Our staff of highly trained professionals—editors, graphic designers, and marketing personnel—work together to produce the very finest book products available. The company reflects in every aspect the philosophy established by the founders based on Psalms 68:11, "The Lord gave the word and great was the company of those who published it."

If you would like further information, please call
1-888-361-9473
or visit our website at
www.tatepublishing.com

Tate Publishing LLC
127 E. Trade Center Terrace
Mustang, Oklahoma 73064 USA